Impact English

MIKE GOULD (SERIES EDITOR), KIM RICHARDSON, MARY GREEN & JOHN MANNION

Key Stage 3 – Year 9 • Student Book 3

Contents

Unit 1 Character assassination

1	The Mazarin Stone by Sir Arthur Conan Doyle	4
	Narrative S1, R15	
2	The Tolkien Disease	11
	Analysis W7, Wr5	
3	Catch Me If You Can: Review	18
	Review Wr7, R8, R12	
4	Assignment: Detective story	24
	Narrative AF1, AF6	

Unit 2 Changing English

1	The Mother Tongue by Bill Bryson	26
	Explanation S11, Wr7, S&L2	
2	Online Words Take Wing	33
	Information S11, Wr7, S&L9	
3	Eats, Shoots and Leaves by Lynne Truss	40
	Argument S10, R11, R12	
4	Assignment: Magazine writer	46
	Argument AF2	

Unit 3 Influential voices

1	Elvis: Why We Love Him, Why We Study Him	48
	Explanation Wr7, Wr10	
2	Presidential Inauguration Speech by Nelson Mandela	55
	Lord Kinnock's Maiden Speech: Parody	56
	Persuasion S7, R12, S&L2	
3	How to Write a Letter to Someone Famous	62
	Advice Wr4, Wr12, Wr15	
4	Assignment: Mobiles for mums	69
	Persuasion AF2	

Unit 4 Inside poetry

1	On the Eighth Day... by Claire Calman	72
	Of Jeoffrey, His Cat by Christopher Smart	77
	Poems S7, S11, Wr8	
2	When We Two Parted by Lord Byron	79
	Anancy's Thoughts on Love by John Agard	81
	Poems S4, R17, Wr17	
3	Homeward Bound by Benjamin Zephaniah	87
	Neighbours by Benjamin Zephaniah	89
	Poems R3, R16, Wr17	
4	Assignment: The critic	95
	Discursive AF2, AF3	

Unit 5 On the streets

1. **Stone Cold: The Play by Joe Standerline** — 98
   Play script — R14, Wr5, S&L14, S&L15
2. **Thames Reach Bondway: Poster and Webpage** — 104
   Persuasion — Wr13, S&L6
3. **As I Walked Out One Midsummer Morning by Laurie Lee** — 111
   Recount — Wr17, S&L12
4. **Assignment: Homeless** — 118
   Recount — AF3, AF4

Unit 6 Your life

1. **Mother and Daughter** — 122
   Discursive — R2, Wr16
2. **Junk Food: Email Forum** — 129
   Argument — Wr14, S&L5
3. **How To… Go To A Party** — 136
   Be Safe at your Firework Party — 137
   Advice — S1, R7, Wr15
4. **Assignment: The Future is bright** — 142
   Argument — AF3

Unit 7 Correspondent

1. **Letter to Daniel by Fergal Keane** — 144
   Recount — R11, Wr11
2. **No Turning Back by Beverley Naidoo** — 150
   Narrative — S4, R1
3. **Tiger Tracking in Rajasthan** — 156
   Information — S9, Wr9
4. **Assignment: Himalaya correspondent** — 163
   Information — AF3

Unit 8 Darkness visible

1. **The Woman in Black by Susan Hill** — 166
   Narrative — W7, S6, R3
2. **What is a Phobia?** — 173
   Information — S2, W6, Wr4
3. **To Kill a Mockingbird: Play by Christopher Sergal** — 179
   To Kill a Mockingbird by Harper Lee — 185
   Play script, Narrative — R10, R14, S&L14
4. **Assignment: Self-help** — 187
   Information — AF2, AF5

Unit 9 Growing pains

1. **The Lost Boys' Appreciation Society by Alan Gibbons** — 190
   Narrative — W7, Wr5
2. **Boys, It Seems, Are At The Top Of The Agenda Again** — 197
   Discursive — W4a, S3, S&L9
3. **Chinese Cinderella by Adeline Yen Mah** — 204
   Autobiography — W7, R6, Wr4
4. **Assignment: The journalist** — 210
   Discursive — AF2, AF4

Unit 10 Practising for Assessment — 212

Unit 1 Character assassination

1 Count Sylvius calls

Aims

- Read an extract from a short story
- Review and develop your writing of more complex sentences (S1)
- Explore how a text reflects the time it was written and what makes it popular today (R15)
- Write about a villainous character

This text is from a short story by Sir Arthur Conan Doyle about the famous detective, Sherlock Holmes.

It was, therefore, an empty room into which Billy, a minute later, ushered Count Sylvius. The famous game-shot, sportsman and man-about-town was a big, swarthy fellow, with a formidable dark moustache, shading a cruel, thin-lipped mouth, and surmounted by a long, curved nose, like the beak of an eagle. He was well dressed, but his brilliant necktie, shining pin and glittering rings were flamboyant in their effect. As the door closed behind him he looked round him with fierce, startled eyes, like one who suspects a trap at every turn. Then he gave a violent start as he saw the impassive head and the collar of the dressing-gown which projected above the armchair in the window. At first his expression was one of pure amazement. Then the light of a horrible hope gleamed in his dark, murderous eyes. He took one more glance round to see that there were no witnesses, and then, on tiptoe, his thick stick half raised, he approached the silent figure. He was crouching for his final spring and blow when a cool, sardonic voice greeted him from the open bedroom door.

   'Don't break it, Count! Don't break it!'

   The assassin staggered back, amazement in his convulsed face. For an instant he half raised his loaded cane once more, as if he would turn his violence from the effigy to the original; but there was something in that steady grey eye and mocking smile which caused his hand to sink to his side.

   'It's a pretty little thing,' said Holmes, advancing towards the image. 'Tavernier, the French modeller, made it. He is as good at waxworks as your friend Straubenzee is at air-guns.'

'Air-guns, sir! What do you mean?'

'Put your hat and stick on the side-table. Thank you! Pray take a seat. Would you care to put your revolver out also? Oh, very good, if you prefer to sit upon it. Your visit is really most opportune, for I wanted badly to have a few minutes' chat with you.'

The Count scowled, with heavy, threatening eyebrows. 'I too, wished to have some words with you, Holmes. That is why I am here. I won't deny that I intended to assault you just now.'

Holmes swung his leg on the edge of the table. 'I rather gathered that you had some idea of the sort in your head,' said he. 'But why these personal attentions?'

'Because you have gone out of your way to annoy me. Because you have put your creatures upon my track.'

'My creatures! I assure you no!'

'Nonsense! I have had them followed. Two can play at that game, Holmes.'

'It is a small point, Count Sylvius, but perhaps you would kindly give me my prefix when you address me. You can understand that, with my routine of work, I should find myself on familiar terms with half the rogues' gallery, and you will agree that exceptions are invidious.'

'Well, Mr Holmes, then.'

'Excellent! But I assure you you are mistaken about my alleged agents.'

Count Sylvius laughed contemptuously. 'Other people can observe as well as you. Yesterday there was an old sporting man. Today it was an elderly woman. They held me in view all day.'

'Really, sir, you compliment me. Old Baron Dowson said the night before he was hanged that in my case what the law had gained the stage had lost. And now you give my little impersonations your kindly praise!'

'It was you – you yourself?'

Holmes shrugged his shoulders. 'You can see in the corner the parasol which you so politely handed to me in the Minories before you began to suspect.'

'If I had known, you might never—'

'Have seen this humble home again. I was well aware of it. We all have neglected opportunities to deplore. As it happens, you did not know, so here we are!'

The Count's knotted brows gathered more heavily over his menacing eyes. 'What you say only makes the matter worse. It was not your agents, but your play-acting, busy-body self! You admit that you have dogged me. Why?'

'Come now, Count. You used to shoot lions in Algeria.'

'Well?'

'But why?'

'Why? The sport – the excitement – the danger!'

'And no doubt, to free the country from a pest?'

'Exactly!'

'My reasons in a nutshell!'

The Count sprang to his feet, and his hand involuntarily moved back to his hip-pocket.

'Sit down, sir, sit down! There was another, more practical reason. I want that yellow diamond!'

Count Sylvius lay back in his chair with an evil smile.

'Upon my word!' said he.

Key Reading

Narrative texts

This text is a **narrative**. Its main **purpose** is to entertain us. The main features of this text are:

- It has a **structure** that includes an **introduction** and the **development** of the plot (the complication, the climax and resolution all come later).

- It uses **expressive** and **descriptive language**, for example, 'The Count *scowled*, with *heavy*, threatening *eyebrows*.'

- It has **characters**, who the story is about. There is also a **narrator**, who tells the story and is either present as a character, in which case it is generally told in the first person (I/we) or is not present, in which case it is told in the third person (he/she/it/they), for example, 'Holmes swung *his* leg on the edge of the table.'

- It uses **dialogue/direct speech** to develop the story, or to tell us about characters and their feelings. For example: '"Sit down, sir, sit down! There was another, more practical reason. I want that yellow diamond!"' (story); '…and now you give my little impersonations your kindly praise!' (character – Holmes is almost mocking the count by being over polite).

1 a) Note down two details about Count Sylvius's face from the first paragraph that create strong images in your mind.

  b) Note down two words or phrases that tell you that Count Sylvius is a villain, not a hero.

2 Count Sylvius believes there is someone else in the room when he enters. What does he plan to do to them?

3 a) What are the first spoken words in this extract? Who is speaking?

b) Look at this line spoken by Count Sylvius. What does it reveal about his character?

> 'Why? The sport – the excitement – the danger!'

4 Count Sylvius thinks that Holmes has employed people to follow him. What has *actually* happened?

Purpose

5 The purpose of the story is to entertain the reader.
In pairs, discuss the different ways in which the writer makes the story entertaining: Think about:
- character description
- tricks or twists in the plot
- suspense or tension
- humour.

Find evidence in the story for what you decide.

Reading for meaning

The Sherlock Holmes stories were written at the end of the 19th century and the start of the 20th – about a hundred years ago.

6 Why do you think they are still read and enjoyed today?

7 If we look at the stories closely, we can see that they reflect the times when they were written.

   a) Look through the text and see if you can find evidence for the following. Copy and complete the table below.

Focus	Example	How this is different now
Vocabulary changes (words or phrases we wouldn't use much now)	'pray' (line 21)	'please'
Changes in the way we live (something that doesn't happen much now)		
References to **objects that are** less common now		

   b) Identify any other examples of language change. Then ask a partner to find the word or phrase in the text and decide on its modern meaning.

· ·

Focus on: Complex sentences and added detail

One example of a **simple sentence** from the text is as follows:

SUBJECT (the person *doing* the action)

Holmes shrugged his shoulders.

VERB (what is being done)   OBJECT (the thing that receives the action)

If the sentence had been written as follows, it would be a **complex sentence**:

Holmes shrugged his shoulders, so that the Count could see he wasn't scared.

The **conjunction** links the **main clause** to the second or **subordinate clause**. This subordinate clause would not make sense on its own.

8 Here are three more simple sentences based on the text. Turn them into complex sentences by adding further information after the conjunction.

  a) Count Sylvius lay back in his chair with an evil smile, *although* he…

  b) Count Sylvius laughed contemptuously, *after* Holmes had…

  c) The Count sprang to his feet, *before* the police…

The key thing to remember is that good writers add **further detail** and **information** to create pictures in the reader's mind. Look at this example:

> As the door closed behind him *he looked round him with fierce, startled eyes*, like one who suspects a trap at every turn.

This sentence does three things:
- It tells us what is happening while the Count is looking around.
- It tells us the fact that he looked around.
- It tells us how he looked around, comparing him to something else.

9 a) Identify which sections in the sentence do each of these three things.

  b) Which of the sections is the **main clause** (i.e. would make sense as a sentence on its own)? Write it down.

  c) What type of comparison is used here (it starts: 'like one who…')?

Exploring further

As has been shown, the main clause may not be the longest part of a sentence, but it is the most important.

10 a) Identify the main clause in this sentence:
'He was well dressed, but his brilliant necktie, shining pin, and glittering rings were flamboyant in their effect.'

  b) Can this sentence be rearranged by moving the main clause? Will the conjunction also move, or should it be replaced with an alternative? (Try using one of these: 'although', 'while', 'yet'.)

Character assassination

Key Writing

11 This story is all about two powerful characters – Sherlock Holmes and Count Sylvius. You are going to create a villain or criminal for a new Sherlock Holmes story.

a) Firstly, make notes on your villain. Describe his or her face using detailed and vivid adjectives, like Conan Doyle does. For example:

'She had a *short, ugly* nose.'

Note down details about more than one feature of his or her face.

b) Then make further notes on different aspects of his or her appearance. If need be, look again at how the writer makes Count Sylvius come to life.

c) The story will start with your villain entering the room, so make notes on their thoughts and actions as they come in.

d) Write the opening paragraph to your story. Try to describe how your villain moves and what his or her thoughts are as well as how he or she looks. Make your description at least 100 words long and pack it with detail. If you can, include one or two complex sentences using a conjunction such as 'although', 'because' or 'so that'.

You could use this example to get you started. Provide extra detail by adding adjectives before 'door', or add impact by selecting a different verb for 'entered'.

> The .... door opened and .... entered. He/she had...

- adjective(s) (size, type of door?)
- name of your villain
- different verb

Exploring further

12 a) How would you describe Holmes's behaviour in the extract on pages 4–5? Write one or two paragraphs trying to sum up succinctly and clearly what he is like. If you can, draw contrasts with Count Sylvius's behaviour. Is one cooler and calmer than the other? Is one more aggressive?

b) Try adding a few lines of dialogue between the two characters to bring out the differences in their characters.

2 The Tolkien disease

> Read part of a biography of a famous author
> Explore how a writer makes a point in an unusual way (W7)
> Look at imaginative ways of beginning an analysis (Wr5)

The following text is from the opening of a biography by Susan Ang about the author J. R. R. Tolkien called *The Master of the Rings*. But has he done something terrible?

J. R. R. Tolkien, author of *The Hobbit* and *The Lord of the Rings*, is perhaps the greatest fantasy writer ever to have lived; he is certainly the most influential. But there is a darker side to this great man. He is also the creator of one of the most dangerous and communicable diseases known to man: Tolkienomania. This disease can be described as follows:

Most often transmitted through reading, although it can also be communicated through other media, such as film. Symptoms: during the initial stages of the disease, patient may suffer loss of appetite and refuse to appear for meals. Eyes will be glazed. Sufferers may turn violent or experience serious anxiety attacks should the next volume not be to hand. In the later stages of the disease, the glazed look disappears, but only to be replaced by a fanatical gleam in the eye. This and the bulging pocket or rucksack – in which will be stored a copy/multiple copies of The Lord of the Rings *with which to infect others – are warnings that the disease is about to be transmitted. No known cure exists.*

Behind this light-heartedness lies a serious point. The chief characteristic of fans of *The Lord of the Rings* (the book) is a single-mindedness about the worth and wonder of the work itself. Even before the Peter Jackson film cast its spell over cinema audiences around the world ('One film to bring them all and in the darkness bind them', as Gandalf might have said), the world was full of Tolkienomanes. In the UK in 1996, the bookshop chain Waterstones ran a poll for the top 100 books of the century. *The Lord of the Rings* topped the poll, beating the likes of George Orwell's *Nineteen Eighty-*

four and J. D. Salinger's *The Catcher in the Rye* (*The Hobbit* came nineteenth). The book itself has never been out of print since its first publication in 1954–5, and has sold over 100 million copies. And for years the world has been full of Tolkien societies, Tolkien criticism, Tolkien webpages and women calling themselves 'Galadriel'.

The film of *The Lord of the Rings* is a very good film. It is all in glorious Technicolour, gives a visual concreteness to Middle-earth, which is at one level very satisfying, and has some breathtaking moments (the Moria sequences are, in particular, quite superb). It is all very enjoyable. But the film is not the book.

What is it that makes the book so great? As Tolkien himself said, *The Lord of the Rings* is primarily an 'exciting story'. That was what he thought the people who had enjoyed it had responded to and this, he said, was how it had been written. But it is not only an exciting story, or rather, it is not just because it is an exciting story that people have been reading it for nearly fifty years. So, what is it about Tolkien's work, in particular *The Lord of the Rings*, which has prompted and continues to prompt such responses? Why does it enthral, excite and, perhaps above all, move readers? What makes it work? There are probably no short answers to these questions. But the fact that his work is read today as avidly, if not more avidly, than it was when it was first published, and has a breadth of appeal clearly shown by its translation into more than thirty-five languages, suggests that *The Lord of the Rings* deals in universals. It would not otherwise have transcended time and culture as it has.

Key Reading

> ### Analysis texts
>
> This text is an **analysis**. Its **purpose** is to look at something that has happened and explore and seek to understand it.
>
> The main features of this text are:
>
> - It separates information and evidence into **clear paragraphs**
>   For example, the first paragraph explains who Tolkien is.
> - It asks and addresses **key questions**, for example, 'What is it that makes the book so great?'
> - It refers to **quotes** and **sources** to back up these questions, for example, 'As Tolkien himself said, *The Lord of the Rings* is primarily an "exciting story"'.
> - It **weighs up evidence** using **connectives** that draw out contrasts. For example, the writer compares the film and the original book: 'But the film is not the book.'

1. The text is divided into several paragraphs. What is the second paragraph (in italics) about?
2. Look at the questions that are asked in the text. Is the author asking the readers to answer them, or are the questions used in a different way?
3. In order to show how great the book is, Susan Ang refers to some evidence – a 'poll' from 1996. Who conducted the poll, and what did it show?
4. Identify the quote in paragraph 3 that Susan Ang has adapted to make a joke.
5. Find another example of the use of 'But…' to show a contrasting point will follow.

Purpose

What is really interesting about this text is that the writer gets our attention in an unusual way by describing 'Tolkienomania' as a disease.

6 Discuss these questions in pairs:

 a) Why is this an unusual way to describe how fans of the book behave?

 b) What are the main symptoms of the 'disease'?

 c) Have you ever felt or acted like this about something?

Reading for meaning

The writer could have just said that the book was very popular and that people couldn't stop themselves reading it. Instead, she uses a **metaphor**. This is when a writer writes about something as if it is something else. In this case: *Loving the book = an addiction, or disease.*

The writer also *exaggerates* to make her point. For example, '…sufferers (fans of the book) may turn violent… should the next volume not be to hand.'

W7 **7** Here are two other metaphors that work in a similar way:
- Your life is a mountain climb.
- Shopping is a medieval battle.

Write down as many things as you can that 'life' or 'shopping' have in common with the metaphor used (for example, you *fight* for bargains).

Exploring further: Exaggerating for effect

One way of livening up a text is to select your nouns carefully. Susan Ang uses the word 'sufferer' rather than 'reader' or 'fan'. She could have used any of the following words that describe people who are emotionally attached to things or people:

fan, supporter, addict, lover (of something), patron, follower.

8 In pairs, discuss how the meaning of each word differs. Then rank them in order of the strength of attachment (for example, 'addict' might be number one on your list).

Another technique writers use is to exaggerate dull things for entertainment. The reader understands that the writer is embroidering the truth and shares the joke with them. For example: 'When the other team came out of the changing room they were all about 15 feet tall, and growled at each other in a language that must have been 'gorilla'.'

9 a) What two exaggerations does the writer make here?

b) What effect do they have on the reader?

Focus on: Imaginative ways of opening texts

The author chose to open her book about J. R. R. Tolkien by making the popularity of *The Lord of the Rings* sound like a medical warning.

However, there are other ways of making the beginning of texts interesting. Susan Ang could have started by asking questions in the first paragraph (she actually asks her questions later). This might work because it could make the reader want to know the answers. For example:

> J. R. R. Tolkien is one of the greatest writers who ever lived. But why are his books so loved? And where did he get his ideas from? What do we really know about this man, and his life?

This technique also leads the reader to believe that the text will answer these questions if they read on. It is common in analysis texts to set out the different aspects of the topic to be analysed at the start of the text.

Often the first question begins with the connective 'But…' to show that ideas that contrast with or challenge the original statement will follow. For example, 'But why are his books so loved?'.

Wr5

10 Come up with a set of questions to add to an opening statement about a favourite team or pop star.

You could start like this:

……are the greatest team ever. But why…?

or

…………is the greatest pop star/band ever. But how…?

Use a range of question starters to add variety. For example:

- Why?
- How?
- Where?
- When?
- What?

Exploring further

Questions in analysis texts are sometimes followed by answers, either in the present tense – saying what the book/article *does* – or the future tense, saying what it *will do*. For example:

Future tense:

> But how did they win so many titles? In this article, I will explore how they built a winning team and what it cost them…

Present tense:

> But how did they win so many titles? In this article, I explore how they built a winning team and what it cost them…

11 In the last paragraph of the text, does Susan Ang use the present or future tense in this way?

Key Writing

12 Now try to imitate Susan Ang's idea about a disease in a description of your favourite football team or pop star.

> 'Gunnermania' is a dreadful disease. It is at its worst on Saturdays when Arsenal play at home. The sufferer leaps out of bed and cannot stop him or herself putting on red and white clothes...

If you are an Arsenal fan, continue the idea above. If you are a fan of another team, adapt it or start a new one.

If you are writing about a pop star you could begin...

> [name of star + 'ania']... is an awful disease. The disease is caught when the sufferer is close to a television and sees their star perform. The first symptom is to grab the remote control when the programme ends and feverishly flick through channels to search for a new fix...

Exploring further

13 Once you have written your first draft, see if you can make it more exaggerated or ridiculous. For example:

'The disease is caught when the sufferer has *their nose pressed up against the TV screen* and sees *their idol prance about* for the first time. The first symptom is clutching the remote control *so hard your veins swell up...*'

14 Another way in which writers exaggerate for effect is to exaggerate numbers or amounts. For example:

'To celebrate watching his/her Arsenal DVD for the *nine hundredth* time, the sufferer insists on wearing all *fifteen of his/her Arsenal kits*. He/she saves up *thousands of pounds* for season tickets for the next *two centuries* so he or she won't miss a game.'

Try adding similar exaggerations to your writing.

 Teenage con man

Aims

- Read a review of a film based on a real criminal's life
- Explore how a non-fiction text can convey information in an interesting way (Wr7)
- Analyse the use of rhetorical devices (R12)
- Write about a scene from a film or television programme

The following text is a review of the film *Catch Me If You Can*.

Catch Me if You Can

Leonardo DiCaprio effortlessly charms his way through Steven Spielberg's zippy, lightweight chase thriller, the real-life tale of con-man extraordinaire Frank Abagnale Jr.

5   It's fortunate that *Catch Me If You Can* is based on a true story, for otherwise film-goers, on exiting cinemas, would be outraged with incredulity at the whole affair. A smart-ass 19-year-old passing himself off as a pilot, a lawyer and a doctor while amassing over $2 million through forged cheques? Yeah, right.

10 But this is all a relatively faithful adaptation of the autobiography of one Frank Abagnale Jr (co-written with Stan Redding), who did indeed pull off all of the above – and much more besides – before the age of 21. Leonardo DiCaprio plays the con man in question. Early scenes see him honing the art of deception even as an adolescent, posing as a substitute
15 teacher and conducting, rather than joining, a French lesson.

    When his parents announce their intention to divorce, the 17-year-old Abagnale Jr is sent reeling into the big wide world, and so begin his four years of top-level scamming. It's not long before his trickery attracts the attention of the FBI, specifically uptight agent Carl Hanratty (Hanks,
20 turning in a subtly nuanced performance in perhaps his least self-indulgent role, well, ever). Cat-and-mouse shenanigans follow and – would you believe it? – the two build up a grudging respect for one another.

This is not a deeply significant Spielberg movie, but, as anyone who sat through every turgid frame of *A.I.* can testify, this is not necessarily a bad thing. What the director does deliver – with the deceptive ease of an old pro – is a lively caper that is pretty compelling throughout.

Beside the film's breeziness, Spielberg and writer Jeff Nathanson work in some depth. Abagnale, despite his jet-set lifestyle, cuts a lonely soul. In one scene he telephones Hanratty on Christmas Eve, ostensibly to taunt him, but in fact – as Hanratty swiftly deduces – because he's got no one else to talk to. But it's the relationship between Abagnale and his father, Frank Sr (Walken), that provides the film's best moments. Walken is magnificent – rendering Frank Sr outwardly upbeat but with despair oozing out of him as he tries to maintain dignity in the face of an IRS investigation.

Yet this is all a sideshow to the main event: Abagnale's relentless scamming. DiCaprio makes a reasonable account of himself in the role, for the most part coming across as effortlessly charismatic (his teenage girl fan club will love the movie). You can't help wishing for the dark undertones of, say, John Cusack in *The Grifters* – after all, when you think about it, posing as a doctor isn't perhaps as much of a laugh as it is portrayed here.

Minor gripes aside, what you're left with is a witty, charming comedy-thriller – *The Sting* for the new millennium (with a jazzy, Mancini-inspired score by John Williams to boot). It's the sort of film that, if it were made 50 years ago, people would observe that 'they don't make 'em like this anymore.' Thankfully, courtesy of Mr Spielberg, they do.

Key Reading

Reviews

This text is a **review.** Its **purpose** is to inform and entertain us. It also tells us what the reviewer thinks of the film.

The main features of this text are:

- It gives **basic information** about the story line, characters, and the people involved, for example, the cast and the director.

- It gives us an idea of what the **reviewer's opinion** is, through the words and phrases selected, for example, 'Minor gripes aside, what you're left with is a *witty, charming* comedy-thriller.'

- It has a **friendly, informal tone** and uses a number of ways to 'connect' with the reader, for example, '…would you believe it?'

- It uses a **wide range of sentences** often packed with **detail,** and uses the **present tense**, for example, 'Early scenes see him honing the art of deception even as an adolescent…'

1. There are three real people mentioned in the introductory paragraph. Who are they? And what have each of them to do with the film?

2. Find another view expressed by the reviewer in paragraph 4. Which words tell you it is an opinion and not a fact?

3. Another actor – John Cusack – and another film are mentioned later in the review. What is the film? And why do you think it is mentioned?

4. Why is the phrase 'cat-and-mouse shenanigans' a good one to use in the review? Who does it refer to, and what does it mean?

Purpose

5 a) The writer wants to give us a good sense of the feel of the film, and what it is like. Look at the final paragraph. How does the reviewer sum up the film?

Look for an adjective + adjective + noun combination, like this:

A dull, pointless thriller

b) Write another adjective + adjective + noun phrase to give a contrasting summary of the film.

Reading for meaning

6 In line 5, why does the reviewer say it is 'fortunate' that this is a true story?

7 Find any descriptions about Frank Abagnale Jr and note them down. Do you think we are supposed to think of him as a villainous or nasty character? Why?

8 Two of the characters who appear in the film are described, in turn, as 'uptight' and 'outwardly upbeat'. Who are these characters, and what do these descriptions tell us about each man?

Exploring further

One of the skills of review writing is to sum up opinion and provide information in single sentences. For example:

Leonardo DiCaprio effortlessly charms his way through Steven Spielberg's zippy, lightweight chase thriller, the real-life tale of con-man extraordinaire Frank Abagnale Jr.

9 Copy this sentence out and then:

a) Underline any words that suggest praise of the film or the people involved in it.

b) Circle words and phrases that provide information about the story or the type of film it is.

Focus on: Rhetorical questions

Rhetorical questions are questions that are asked for effect and do not require an answer. There are a number of rhetorical questions in the review. For example:

> A smart-ass 19-year-old passing himself off as a pilot, a lawyer and a doctor while amassing over $2 million through forged cheques? Yeah, right.

Through this question the writer puts himself in the shoes of the audience. He is saying: 'If this wasn't a true story would we believe it? No!'

A second rhetorical question is used is when the reviewer describes how the two men – the agent and the con-man – come to respect each other:

> Cat-and-mouse shenanigans follow and – would you believe it? – the two build up a grudging respect for one another.

10 a) Why is this second rhetorical question used? What effect does it have on the reader?

b) What punctuation does the reviewer use to draw attention to the rhetorical question, and why?

Rhetorical questions can be used in lots of other ways – for example, to express anger or disgust:

- 'Are these terrorists really interested in freedom?'
- 'Do you really expect me to forgive you for what you have done?'

11 Complete the following rhetorical questions:

- Police officer to a teenager carrying four mobile phones:
  'So, am I supposed to believe that…?'
- Sports commentator as an athlete pulls out of a race:
  'She's clearly exhausted, but if she gives up now we have to ask what will she do, where…?'
- Politician after he is accused of having an affair:
  'Do you really think that I, a married… ?'

Key Writing

One of the ways in which the reviewer makes his review interesting is by giving us small glimpses of scenes from the movie. Here, he describes con-man DiCaprio making a call to Tom Hanks:

> In one scene he telephones Hanratty on Christmas Eve, ostensibly to taunt him, but in fact – as Hanratty swiftly deduces – because he's got no one else to talk to.

12 Take any scene from a television programme or film you have watched recently. Then, using the present tense, describe what happens in two or three sentences. Try to add what it means. You will need to use:

- precise verbs and adverbs
- adjective + adjective + noun phrases
- the names of the characters
- conjunctions to link clauses, such as 'but' or 'although'.

For example:

'In one scene, the ever-troublesome Paul tries to win Lee back by promising faithfully to give up dealing drugs, <u>but</u> we know that he is only faking it – he doesn't really mean it.'

Exploring further

13 a) Try rewriting your scene summary using at least one rhetorical question to involve the reader. Complete this example first:

'In one scene, the ever-troublesome Paul tries to win Lee back by promising to give up dealing drugs, but would you believe a...?'

b) You will also notice the use of adverbs in summing up characters' behaviour (how DiCaprio 'effortlessly *charms*' and Paul is '*promising* faithfully.').
If you haven't already done so, try to use a simple verb + adverb combination like this in your summary?

4 Unit 1 Assignment: Detective story

Assessment Focuses

- AF1 Write imaginative, interesting and thoughtful texts
- AF6 Write with technical accuracy of syntax and punctuation in phrases, clauses and sentences

> **You:** are a writer of detective and mystery stories. A local school has asked you to send in part of one of your best stories for its pupils to finish.
>
> **Your task:** Write the opening and middle sections of the story. The opening must include the detective or the villain, or both. It must also contain some direct speech.

Stage 1

Plan your opening and include some ideas of how the plot will unfold in the middle section.

Make brief notes about:

- your main character's appearance (include strong adjectives)
- where the story begins, for example, in a modern flat, on a station platform or on a rooftop
- what happens in your opening, for example, the detective gets a visit to his or her flat late one night
- what is going to happen later, although this may not be revealed in your opening.

Do not reveal or write an ending to the story.

Stage 2

Draft your first paragraph.

- Make sure you describe clearly what your character is doing. Use your notes to tell the reader what your character looks like. Try to suggest how your character is feeling.
- Write in the past tense and in the third person, for example:
  'Inspector Mortimer answered the door. In front of him stood a tall man holding a gun.'
- If you use dialogue here, or in your other paragraphs, use both direct and indirect speech to add variety to your writing. Make sure you set it out accurately and that it adds interest to what you write.
- Also, consider how you can use punctuation to affect meaning. For example, in 'I had him rattled!', the exclamation mark might suggest the writer is laughing to himself.

Draft at least three more paragraphs to complete your opening.

Stage 3

Now draft the middle section of your story, using the same techniques as listed in Stage 2. Remember to:
- move the story towards a key moment or climax
- develop the character of the villain and your detective
- change the scene or setting, if appropriate
- continue to use direct and indirect speech where necessary
- include detailed description of characters' appearance, behaviour, etc.

Challenge

Make your opening even more interesting by using more than one narrator. Try writing one paragraph as if told by the detective character, then the next as if told by your villain/criminal.

Unit 2 Changing English

① How words are formed

Aims

- Read an explanation text
- Discuss the process it describes (S&L2)
- Examine how it creates tone
- Express your own opinions (S&L2)

Read the following extract from Bill Bryson's book about the English Language, *Mother Tongue*. In this section he is discussing how words are formed.

WORDS ARE CREATED BY ADDING OR SUBTRACTING SOMETHING.

English has more than a hundred common prefixes and suffixes -*able*, -*ness*, -*ment*, *pre*-, *dis*-, *anti*-, and so on – and with these it can form and re-form words with a facility that yet again sets it apart from other tongues. For example, we can take the French word *mutin* (rebellion) and
5   turn it into *mutiny, mutinous, mutinously, mutineer,* and many others, while the French have still just the one form, *mutin*.

    Some word endings are surprisingly rare. If you think of *angry* and *hungry,* you might conclude that *-gry* is a common ending, but in fact it occurs in no other common words in English. Similarly *-dous* appears in
10   only *stupendous, horrendous, tremendous, hazardous,* and *jeopardous,* while *-lock* survives only in *wedlock* and *warlock* and *-red* only in *hatred* and *kindred*. *Forgiveness* is the only example of a verb + *-ness* form. Equally some common-seeming prefixes are actually more rare than superficial thought might lead us to conclude. If you think of *forgive,*
15   *forget, forgo, forbid, forbear, forlorn, forsake,* and *forswear,* you might think that *for-* is a common prefix, but in fact it appears in no other

common words, though once it appeared in scores of others. Why certain forms like *-ish, -ness, -ful,* and *-some* should continue to thrive while others like *-lock* and *-gry* that were once equally popular should fall into disuse is a question without a good answer.

Fashion clearly has something to do with it. The suffix *-dom* was long in danger of disappearing, except in a few established words like *kingdom,* but it underwent a resurgence (largely instigated in America) in the last century, giving us such useful locutions as *officialdom* and *boredom* and later more contrived forms like *best-sellerdom*. The ending *-en* is today one of the most versatile ways we have of forming verbs from adjectives *(harden, loosen, sweeten,* etc.) and yet almost all such words are less than 300 years old.

The process is still perhaps the most prolific way of forming new words and often the simplest. For centuries we had the word *political,* but by loading the single letter *a* on to the front of it, a new word, *apolitical,* joined the language in 1952.

Still other words are formed by lopping off their ends. *Mob,* for example, is a shortened form of *mobile vulgus* (fickle crowd). *Exam, gym,* and *lab* are similar truncations, all of them dating only from the last century when syllabic amputations were the rage. Yet the impulse to shorten words is an ancient one. Indeed, many of our most common words are contractions of whole phrases – for instance, *goodbye,* a shortening of God-be-with-you, and *hello,* which was in Old English *hal beo thu* or 'whole be thou'.

Finally, but no less importantly, English possesses the ability to make new words by fusing compounds – *airport, seashore, footwear, wristwatch, landmark, flowerpot,* and so on almost endlessly. All Indo-European languages have the capacity to form compounds. Indeed, German and Dutch do it, one might say, to excess. But English does it more neatly than most other languages, eschewing the choking word chains that bedevil other Germanic languages and employing the nifty refinement of making the elements reversible, so that we can distinguish between a houseboat and a boathouse, between basketwork and a workbasket, between a casebook and a bookcase. Other languages lack this facility.

Key Reading

Explanation texts

This text is an **explanation** text. Its **purpose** is to explain how a process works in an entertaining manner.

The main features of this text are:

- It has a series of **clear and logical steps** which may include a topic sentence to introduce each step, for example, 'Some word endings are surprisingly rare.'

- It uses **examples** to illustrate the point being explained, such as: 'Forgiveness is the only example of a verb+ -*ness* form.'

- It uses **sentence signposts** to organise and link points clearly, for example, 'Still other words are formed…'

- It uses the **present tense**, when the text is explaining how or why something is now, for example, 'the French *have* still just the one form, mutin.'

- It uses **precise vocabulary**, including technical terms, for example: 'All *Indo-European* languages have the capacity to form *compounds*.'

- It uses **causal language** to show the effect of certain points made, for example, 'Why certain forms…'

1 a) Identify the topic sentence that presents the main point in paragraph 3.
b) How does this link back to paragraph 2?

2 Find an example of a sentence written in the past tense. Why is this tense used at this point?

3 Some of the examples in the text give unexpected information on familiar words. Choose two examples of this.

4 Which words in the last paragraph show the final cause of the language's ability to make new words?

Purpose

The purpose of this text is to explain and to entertain. The challenge of writing this text is that it is telling the reader about something they are already familiar with – their own language.

5 In pairs, discuss how well the text both explains and entertains. Consider how Bryson:

- provides unusual examples
- reveals surprising things that we might not have thought about
- uses playful comments.

Reading for meaning

6 a) As well as the use of prefixes and suffixes, name the two other word forming processes that are presented in the extract.

b) In which paragraphs does Bryson introduce each of these processes?

7 a) What is the mystery about some prefixes and suffixes?

b) Read paragraphs 2 and 3 again, this time listing the examples provided under two headings:

- Prefixes/suffixes found in many words
- Prefixes/suffixes only found in a few words.

Be careful not to confuse *commonly used* with *used in many words*.

8 a) What does Bryson mean by 'syllabic amputations'? Find another term to describe them.

b) Give the full version of these 'syllabic amputations':

- photo
- temp
- pro-am
- demo
- memo
- veg

c) Can you think of any more?

9 Of the three word-forming processes explained, which produces the most words? Which paragraph makes this clear?

10 a) What is clever about the way that English compound words work?

b) How do compound words in English differ from those in other Germanic languages?

Exploring further: Suffixes and prefixes

11 Use the examples given in the extract to deduce the meaning of the following prefixes and suffixes:

- '-ness'
- '-ish'
- '-dom'
- 'for-'
- 'a-'

Refer to an etymological dictionary if you need to.

Focus on: Tone

One of the risks of writing an explanation that is packed full of information is that it can be rather 'dry'. In order to make it more interesting, Bill Bryson has added an element of commentary to his explanation. This involves two main techniques:

- He makes remarks that English is superior to other European languages.
- He shows his admiration for the English language.

12 Note down examples from the text where Bill Bryson comments that English is better than

a) French

b) other Germanic languages.

13 Explain in your own words, using the evidence from the text, how English is:

a) better than French

b) better than other Germanic languages.

14 In pairs, go through the text and collect examples of Bryson's positive statements about English. Record your findings in a table like the one below:

Statement	What it shows about the author's attitude
'it can form and re-form words with a facility that yet again sets it apart from other tongues'	He thinks English forms words more easily than other languages.

15 Look closely at the following words in bold, taken from a sentence in the final paragraph. In this case Bryson interweaves his comments as he explains one of his points.

> ...eschewing the **choking** word **chains** that **bedevil** other Germanic languages and employing the **nifty refinement** of making the elements reversible...

a) What does Bill Bryson's choice of words here show about his attitude to 'other Germanic' languages?

b) What does his choice of words here show about his attitude to English?

16 Do you think Bill Bryson makes these remarks because:
- he genuinely believes them
- he wants to draw comparisons between European languages
- he wishes to flatter English readers
- a combination of the above.

Explain your choices with evidence from the extract.

17 In pairs, discuss whether you think Bryson's enthusiasm works. Do you feel more positive about English after reading this passage? Or do you feel the other languages have been misrepresented?

Exploring further: Informal touches

In the example above, Bryson's pairing of 'nifty' with 'refinement' shows how he occasionally brings an informal tone to his explanation. His aim is to make it more user-friendly by balancing out terms like 'eschewing' that appear earlier in the sentence.

18 Try replacing the word 'nifty' with each of the following to see what effect it has on the tone of the sentence:
- clever
- technical
- neat
- deft.

Key Writing

The challenge of writing about language is that readers may believe that they already know what you are telling them, so the way that explanation is presented becomes more important.

19 In pairs, discuss the key facts given below for the process behind 'why we have day and night' and 'why days vary in length through the year'.

- Earth rotates round the Sun once per year
- Earth rotates on its own axis once every 24 hours
- Day is when the earth faces the Sun
- Night is when we are in the earth's own shadow
- Shorter days in the winter are caused by the Earth being tilted away from the Sun
- Longer days in the summer are caused by the Earth being tilted towards the Sun
- What it would be like if there was not 24 hour rotation

a) How would you present an explanation interestingly and enthusiastically to an audience of people of your own age? Think about:

- your choice of language – include a few comments on the facts you are introducing
- your ordering of the main points and how you will link them – use causal language and sentence signposts
- your choice of examples – select the most interesting
- your tone – include a few informal words or phrases to vary the tone.

b) Write a brief explanation text based on these facts. You could begin:

'The miracle of day and night is not often appreciated, especially by those of us who can't get up in the morning.'

2 Online words

Aims

- Read an information text
- Discuss the ideas it raises (S11)
- Examine methods of presentation (Wr7)
- Express your own opinions (S&L9)

Read the following newspaper article about the role of the Internet in the development of the English Language.

ONLINE WORDS TAKE WING

Our vocabulary is constantly being enriched, but the web is now accelerating the process. Robbie Hudson hails a new word order.

New things have always needed naming, of course, and 'googling', 'blog' and 'fanfic' are essentially phenomenona of the Internet rather than indications of any great transformation of the language. Indeed, Eric S Raymond, the presiding eminence at *The Jargon File* (www.catb.org/~esr/jargon), a dictionary devoted to the vocabulary of the techie community, doubts that there has been an increase in linguistic ingenuity, but he adds that 'pre-Internet, a much higher percentage was never captured in any equivalent of an archive'.

This is crucial because, for a word to enter the language permanently, it must be written down. The OED website notes that of the many words credited to Shakespeare, some were terms he was merely the first person to record in a form that has survived. The web is revolutionising how this happens today by disseminating new words at lightning speed and storing them in searchable archives.

Fiona McPherson, a senior editor at the OED who deals with new words, explains that she has to be enormously careful because, 'once a word makes the dictionary, it is there for ever'. She adds that the dictionary is not a comprehensive list of all words ever used, because language is a living thing. 'As soon as anyone uses a new word to communicate, it is part of the language, but we aim to include all words that achieve a degree of permanency.'

The Internet is an intrinsically verbal medium, and full of people who are fascinated by words. As well as such dictionaries as The Jargon File, there are dozens of sites devoted to spotting neologisms — one of the best being The Word Spy, which Fiona McPherson certainly keeps in her sights. She also refers to web databases to find words she can follow to printed records (OED editors are extremely unhappy about citing online sources that might disappear at the flick of a switch).

In addition, the number of times a word appears in a search engine gives a rough guide to how widely it is used, though this is a blunt instrument and might simply show that one substantial source is keen on that word; McPherson explains that words generally merit consideration only when they achieve both breadth (typically five separate written sources) and endurance (typically five years).

In pre-Internet times, compiling a new edition of the OED was such a herculean undertaking that only two have been published in 75 years — along with a few volumes of additions. Inevitably, some words slipped through the cracks. The online version has made updating easier, with something like 200 words added every quarter. The editors' standards have not dropped a jot, but the explosion of archives online means that words used by quite private groups have become more permanent and widespread.

[George Bush's] use of 'misunderestimate' has a chance of making the OED because the dictionary is descriptive, not prescriptive. It is the historical record of a living language, and, as Jesse Sheidlower of the OED points out: 'We are not the Academie Francaise. The Internet, which spreads misunderstandings as quickly as everything else, helps to solidify misusage as well as usage. If a speech by the president of the USA, who has degrees from Harvard and Yale, isn't indicative of use, then what is?'

Giving new words permanency enriches the language.

Key Reading

> ### Information texts
>
> This is an **information** text. Its **purpose** is to inform the reader about something.
>
> The main features of this text are:
>
> - It contains both **general statements** and **specific facts** organised in a **logical order**, for example, '…for a word to enter the language permanently, it must be written down' and 'The OED website notes that of the many words credited to Shakespeare…'
> - It uses the **present tense** when telling things as they are now, for example, 'The Internet *is* an intrinsically verbal medium…'
> - It uses **specialist vocabulary**, for example, 'descriptive, not prescriptive…'
> - It uses **formal** and **impersonal language**, for example, 'we aim to include all words that achieve a degree of permanency.'

1. Which phrase in paragraph 3 shows the logical link back to paragraph 1?

2. Identify three words in this text which you think did not exist ten years ago.

3. **a)** Find a rare example of the past tense in paragraph 7.

   b) Why has it been used here?

4. **a)** Which words and phrases make the following sentence both formal and impersonal?

> In pre-Internet times, compiling a new edition of the OED was such a herculean undertaking that only two have been published in 75 years…

   b) What effect does this formal style of language have on the reader?

5. Why do you think the author chose the example of George Bush to illustrate his argument about how words get into dictionaries?

Purpose

6 With a partner, discuss what you think the purpose of this text is:
- to help people to understand how new words become permanent
- to give information about how the Internet is speeding up the process of entry of new words into the language.

Provide detailed evidence for your choice from the text.

7 Decide together who the main audience is for this text:
- the on-line 'techie' community
- newspaper readers in general
- language specialists.

What clues in the text support your decision?

Reading for meaning

8 a) What must happen to a new word before it can enter the English language permanently?

b) How long do dictionary makers wait before they decide a word is permanent? And how many written sources do they require?

9 a) What is wrong with the word 'misunderestimate'? How could it have been rephrased? What other words might have been meant here?

b) Why might misunderestimate eventually reach the dictionary?

10 a) Explain as clearly as you can the difference between a descriptive and a prescriptive dictionary.

b) Which of these approaches does the Academie Francaise take?

11 In your own words, explain how the Internet is of help to dictionary makers.

12 In pairs, look back at each paragraph of the text and find the key words or topic sentence. Write these down.

13 a) Use these topic sentences in a spidergram to show the shape of the text. Follow the example begun below:

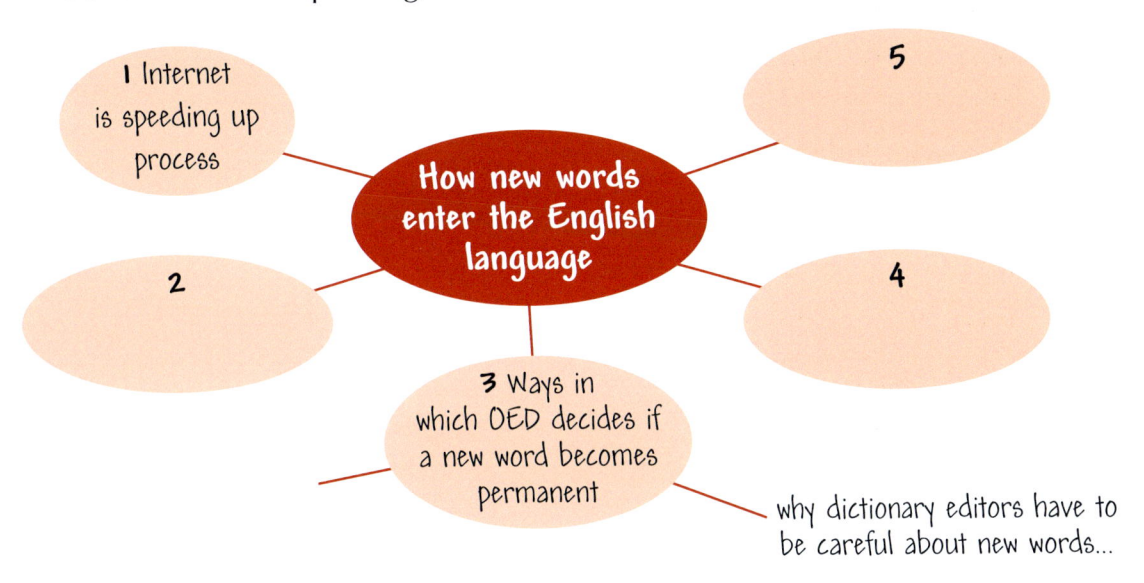

- 1 Internet is speeding up process
- 2
- **How new words enter the English language**
- 3 Ways in which OED decides if a new word becomes permanent
- 4
- 5
- why dictionary editors have to be careful about new words...

b) From your completed plan, what do you notice about the way paragraph breaks relate to each main point or section of the text?

c) Try reordering the main points to see if there is another logical way of presenting the information contained in the article. Be ready to discuss your ideas.

Focus on: Specialist vocabulary

Every subject area has its own specialist vocabulary. In some subjects this is very obvious.

14 Can you identify the areas that these words belong to?

a) Chemotherapy
b) Highest common factor
c) Erosion
d) Inertia
e) Monotheism
f) Catalyst

In other areas the specialist vocabulary is less obvious. In English-language studies, for example, 'word' could be seen as a specialist term.

15 Fill in the table below with examples of specialist vocabulary from different areas and their ordinary meanings.

Word	Ordinary meaning	Specialist meaning	Area of knowledge
hard drive			computing
mass			physics
sum			maths
sentence			criminology
entry			dictionaries
bug			computing

Specialist vocabulary is fine when all the readers are specialists, but it causes problems when a general audience is being addressed.

16 In pairs, look again at the specialist terms in paragraph 2. How many did you know without looking them up in a dictionary?

17 Apart from providing a glossary, how else could the writer help the reader with unfamiliar terms?

The most common way of providing help with specialist vocabulary is to provide explanations as you go along. For example:

> Erosion (the gradual wearing away of rock by wind and water) helps to shape the landscape.

One potential problem with this is that the explanations can start to get in the way of understanding the basic information.

18 a) With your partner discuss whether bracketed explanations or glossaries are the best method for helping a reader with specialist terms.

b) Write a list of the advantages and disadvantages of these two methods and then decide on your answer.

Exploring further: Footnotes

Another way in which specialist terms could be explained is by using **footnotes**. These give extra information at the bottom of a page or paragraph. A number or an asterisk in the text tells the reader where to find the footnote. An example from the article would look like this:

'New things have always needed naming, of course, and "googling"[1], "blog"[2] and 'fanfic'[3] are essentially…'

1 Searching the Internet using the 'Google' search engine

19 What are the advantages of using footnotes over glossaries or bracketed explanations in the text?

Key Writing

There is a famous story of how the word 'quiz' came about. Two men had a bet to see if they could introduce a new word into English. They decided on the word 'quiz' for their experiment and the one man had it written up on walls around the city of Dublin. People naturally asked what this word meant and thus began the modern meaning of the word.

20 a) Using the information you have gained from the text, write an article aimed at teenagers on how they can get one of their favourite but little-known words into the dictionary.

In pairs, brainstorm ideas for your information text. Choose your word carefully, it should be either useful or original (for example, a word used by skateboarders or a word used by a group of friends). Then summarise your main points in a spidergram like the one to the right.

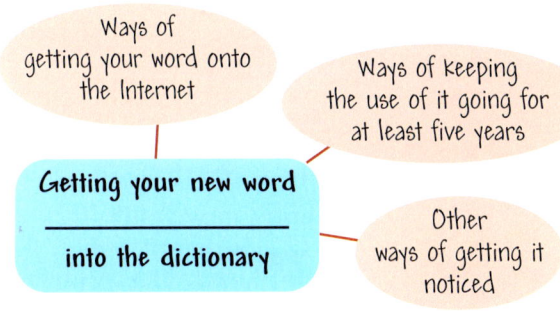

Spidergram: **Getting your new word into the dictionary** — Ways of getting your word onto the Internet; Ways of keeping the use of it going for at least five years; Other ways of getting it noticed.

b) On your own, decide how you will split your main points into paragraphs. One bubble might make one or two paragraphs.

c) Write your short information text, remembering to:
- write in the present tense
- use formal language but also include some informal phrases (remember your audience)
- use some specialist vocabulary (decide which terms need explaining and whether you will used a glossary, brackets or footnotes to present these)
- provide examples of successful word creation.

3 Punctuation makes sense

Aims

- Read an extract from an argument text
- Develop the skill of looking for key ideas
- Look at the author's use of emotive language (R12)
- Write your own argument

Read the following text. It is from the introduction to the best-selling book about punctuation, *Eats, Shoots and Leaves*. In it the author, Lynne Truss, explains how she became obsessed with words and punctuation.

While other girls were out with boyfriends on Sunday afternoons, getting their necks disfigured by love bites, I was at home with the wireless listening to an Ian Messiter quiz called *Many a Slip*, in which erudite and amusing contestants spotted grammatical errors in pieces of prose. It was a fantastic programme. I dream sometimes they have brought it back. Panellists such as Isobel Barnett and David Nixon would interrupt Roy Plomley with a buzz and say 'Tautology!' Around this same time, when other girls of my age were attending the Isle of Wight Festival and having abortions, I bought a copy of Eric Partridge's *Usage and Abusage* and covered it in sticky-backed plastic so that it would last a lifetime (it has). Funny how I didn't think any of this was peculiar at the time, when it was behaviour with 'Proto Stickler' written all over it. But I do see now why it was no accident that I later wound up as a sub-editor with a literal blue pencil.

But to get back to those dark-side-of-the-moon years in British education when teachers upheld the view that grammar and spelling got in the way of self-expression, it is arguable that the timing of their grammatical apathy could not have been worse. In the 1970s, no educationist would have predicted the explosion in universal written communication caused by the personal computer, the Internet and the key-pad of the mobile phone. But now, look what's happened: everyone's a writer! Everyone is posting film reviews on Amazon that go like this:

I watched this film [About a Boy] a few days ago expecting the usual hugh Grant bumbling ... character Ive come to loathe/expect over the years. I was thoroughly suprised. This film was great, one of the best films i have seen in a long time. The film focuses around one man who starts going to a single parents meeting, to meet women, one problem He doesnt have a child.

Isn't this sad? People who have been taught nothing about their own language are (contrary to educational expectations) spending all their leisure hours attempting to string sentences together for the edification of others. And there is no editing on the Internet! Meanwhile, in the world of text messages, ignorance of grammar and punctuation obviously doesn't affect a person's ability to communicate messages such as "C U later". But if you try anything longer, it always seems to turn out much like the writing of the infant Pip in *Great Expectations*:

MI DEER JO I OPE U R KRWITE WELL I OPE I SHAL SON B HABELL 4 2 TEEDGE U JO AN THEN WE SHORL B SO GLODD AN WEN I M PRENGTD 2 U JO WOT LARX AN BLEVE ME INF XN PIP.

Changing English

Key Reading

Argument texts

This text is an **argument**. Its **purpose** is to convince the reader of a particular point of view.

The main features of this text are:

- It presents a **series of points** backed up by **reasons or evidence**, for example, the point about the Internet causing more people to write is backed up by an example of an Internet film review.

- It uses **topic sentences** to introduce each main point, for example, 'While other girls were out with boyfriends…I was at home with the wireless…'

- It uses **formal language** but with some **informal** language for effect, for example, 'No educationist would have predicted…' and 'Funny how I didn't think any of this was peculiar…'

- It uses a mainly **reasonable tone** but occasionally a **highly emotive** one, for example, 'Isn't this sad?' and 'attending the Isle of Wight Festival and having abortions…'

- It uses **impersonal language** including the **passive** to bring authority to the argument, for example, 'it is arguable that'.

1 Identify the topic sentence in paragraph 2. Remember topic sentences do not always come early in the paragraph.

2 This text contains a mixture of formal and informal language. Find one example of each.

3 What attitude to British education in the 1970s does the author show when she calls that era the 'dark-side-of-the-moon years'?

4 How is the author trying to affect the reader's feelings when she asks the question 'Isn't this sad?' How would the effect be different if she had written 'Isn't this bad?'

5 a) There is an example of the passive form in the penultimate paragraph. How does this help Lynne Truss's argument?

b) Find another example of impersonal language in the final paragraph.

Purpose

The purpose of this explanation text is to argue for more attention to spelling and grammar. It does this with a combination of personal statements and more formal arguments.

6 In pairs, discuss how the writer presents herself in the personal statements.
- Does she seem better or worse than the girls she grew up with?
- Is her interest in grammar made to sound exciting or slightly sad?

7 How well does the writer's argument about grammar work?
- Do you think there is more 'writing' in everyday life now than in the 1970s?
- Do you think people need to improve their written expression because of this?

Be prepared to report your ideas back to the class

Reading for meaning

8 Does paragraph 1 tell the reader more about:
- what Lynne Truss was interested in the 1960s

or
- what the general interest in grammar was in the 1960s?

9 What reason is given in paragraph 2 for why grammar and spelling were not taught in the 1970s?

10 What developments have happened since to make grammar and spelling more important?

11 How does the author show that she thinks it is a pity that there is no editing on the Internet?

12 What piece of evidence is used to support the writer's argument that spelling and grammar are important in longer text messages?

Exploring further

13 Can you explain what is wrong with the passage quoted by Lynne Truss (lines 25–30)? Copy it down and annotate it.

Punctuation makes sense

14 Now try to translate Pip's early writing into correct English.

> MI DEER JO I OPE U R KRWITE WELL I OPE I SHAL SON B HABELL 4 2 TEEDGE U JO AN THEN WE SHORL B SO GLODD AN WEN I M PRENGTD 2 U JO WOT LARX AN BLEVE ME INF XN PIP.

Note: In *Great Expectations* Pip wanted to be 'apprenticed' to Joe. The last line would be 'In affection, Pip.'

Focus on: Emotive language

Although her argument is logical, the writer's feelings about correct grammar and spelling are also made very plain.

15 a) In pairs, look through the extract and make a list of as many positive statements about language as you can.

b) Now make a list of some of the negative statements

c) Who or what are the negative statements applied to?

16 What do the two main pieces of evidence suggest about people who don't care about grammar and spelling?

17 Consider each of the statements in the table below. Then complete column 2 to suggest how each is meant to affect the reader's feelings.

Statement from argument	How it is meant to affect the reader
Girls … getting their necks disfigured by love bites	
erudite and amusing contestants spotted grammatical errors	
I dream sometimes they have brought it back	
other girls of my age were attending the Isle of Wight Festival and having abortions	
covered it in sticky-backed plastic so that it would last a lifetime (it has)	
the timing of their grammatical apathy could not have been worse	
People … spending all their leisure hours attempting to string sentences together	
like the writing of the infant Pip	

Exploring further: Neutral language

If the emotive words and phrases are removed from an argument, it reduces the language to a more neutral form and can make the intended effect clearer. For example, a neutral form of lines 1–2 would be:

> While other girls were out on Sunday afternoons, getting love bites from their boyfriends…

18 a) Identify what emotive words have been removed and how the sentence has been reordered.

  b) Choose two more statements from the table on page 44 and rewrite them so that they are as neutral as possible.

Key Writing

19 Your task is to write a letter to a music magazine in which you argue that the pop charts do not reflect the best music.

  a) Begin by brainstorming your main arguments in small groups.

  b) On your own, select from your brainstorm the four main arguments you will use. Try to add reasons or evidence alongside to support them.

  c) Draft your letter, remembering to:
  - invent the name of the person you are writing to (for example, 'Dear DJ Whiz…')
  - use a reasonable tone to put across your main points
  - highlight key points and reasons with emotive language to make your feelings clear
  - use some formal and impersonal language to give weight to your argument
  - introduce some informal phrases to keep your reader interested and lighten the tone.

④ Unit 2 Assignment: Magazine writer

Assessment Focus

› AF2 Produce texts which are appropriate to task, reader and purpose

> **You:** are a magazine columnist.
>
> **Your task:** to write an argument explaining that English is not getting worse but is just changing with the times, aimed at older readers who complain about declining standards of English.

Stage 1

Think carefully about the content of your argument. Here are some ideas to help you generate your main points:

- English has always changed: for example, Britain has been invaded time and time again; new continents discovered and new words brought back by explorers.

- Changes still happening – advance of technology; speed with which new words are being thought up and taken up on Internet/mobile phones/e-mail.

- Best way is to adapt to these changes – then they won't seem so bad.

- Is there anything to worry about? Project to the future: how might the language change further?

Use ideas and examples from the texts on pages 26–27 and 33–34 to add reasons and pieces of evidence for to each of your arguments. For example:

> Language is constantly changing: the Old English greeting 'Whole be thou' has morphed in the last 1000 years into our 'Hello'. There is no reason for these changes to stop...

Stage 2

Now plan your argument. Select the four best points for your article and arrange them as numbered points down the page. Consider your audience and how you might influence their views using emotive language.

- What sort of things would appeal to your audience? (For example, taking pride in the language; using spelling and punctuation accurately.)
- How do you show that you understand their feelings? (For example, reassuring words.)
- How do you make them change their ideas? (For example, positive phrases about recent changes to the language.)

Add these ideas to your plan, linking them to the main points with leader lines.

Stage 3

Draft your article, using your plan, but adding any new ideas or phrases that occur to you as you write. Remember to:

- include a topic sentence in each paragraph to signal a new point or idea.
- keep your tone reasonable most of the time
- use emotive language occasionally to help convince your audience
- match the formality of your language to your older audience
- use some informal phrases to set them at ease.

Challenge

Read your draft, looking carefully at the reasons and evidence you have given for each main point.

- Are the main points organised well?
- Are some pieces of supporting evidence weaker than others? Could they be replaced by something stronger?
- Have reasons and pieces of evidence been linked to the main points in the most effective way? Can you find a neater way of relating them?

Make any changes necessary as you redraft your article.

Unit 2 Assignment

Unit 3 Influential voices

1 Elvis the King

Aims

- Read a passage about Elvis Presley
- Explore how non-fiction texts can entertain the audience (Wr7)
- Explain why your own favourite singer is so great (Wr10)

This is the opening passage of a book about Elvis Presley, the 'King' of rock and roll by Frank Coffey.

ELVIS: Why We Love Him, Why We Study Him

Elvis is called 'the King' because he was the flashpoint, the linchpin, the centrepiece of a musical and cultural revolution called rock and roll. It can be said that the rock revolution went on to become the most significant worldwide cultural phenomenon of the 20th century, affecting
5 style, language, art, film, customs, values, ethics, as well as music. Elvis Presley started the revolution.

Elvis Presley made musical and social history by combining heretofore primarily black forms of music – rhythm and blues (R 'n' B) and gospel – with primarily white forms of music – country-and-western and pop – to
10 create a whole new thing called rock.

Of course, Elvis wasn't the only singer bringing rock to the mass American audience. But it was Elvis Presley, preternaturally handsome, sneeringly sexy, with a voice both raw and velvety, who captured the hearts and minds (and loins) of mainstream America. Elvis started out as
15 a pretender to the throne and became the King.

Need another way to get a handle on the King? Think of The Beatles. Like Elvis, the boys from Liverpool (who were huge Elvis fans – even idolisers) radically changed music and culture. Girls swooned, parents raged. Elvis gave us pompadours and sideburns; The Beatles, long locks
20 and facial hair. Elvis was rebellion, '50s style: fast cars and hot nights.

The Beatles provided the late '60s/early '70s version: peace, love and consciousness alteration. But they shared one thing: impact. It's not too grandiose to say that everyone in America was affected by Elvis and The Beatles. Everyone. But Elvis was first.

Elvis died early, at age 42. And, subsequently, something highly improbable happened to Elvis Aaron Presley: The King became bigger in death than in life. Today, Elvis is ubiquitous. A million fans make an annual pilgrimage to his Memphis home, Graceland. Elvis made more money in the three years after his death than during his entire career. He has sold over one billion records.

Elvis impersonators — fanatical fans making careers out of paying homage — are legion, and have become a cultural phenomenon in their own right. (Comedian Andy Kaufman garnered attention with his uncanny impersonation in the 1970s, and today many impersonators actually make a living doing the King Thing.) Supposed sightings of Elvis alive are regularly reported (and joked about) in the media. Elvis collectables are among the most expensive and sought-after trophies in high-toned auction houses in New York, Los Angeles and London. (His American Express card sold for $80,000!) Elvis Presley Enterprises, run by his ex-wife Priscilla to market his name, is a hugely successful business. Elvis's image is on clocks, calendars, mugs, stamps, plates, toys, you name it. You can't avoid Elvis. Twenty years after his death, he is, as the saying goes, everywhere.

In the beginning, there was Elvis. The father of a generation's music. To know him is to know the most influential art form of the 20th century — rock and roll. To understand him is to understand the country: innocent and calculating, vibrant and vulnerable, powerful and flawed — envied and admired around the world.

Elvis Presley left this life in 1977 at age 42. But he will never die.

Long live the King.

> **THE KING AND I**
> "Before Elvis, there was nothing."
> — John Lennon

> **THE KING AND I**
> "There have been contenders, but there is only one King."
> — Bruce Springsteen

Key Reading

> **Explanation texts**
>
> This is an **explanation** text. Its **purpose** is to explain how or why something is as it is.
>
> The main features of this text are:
>
> - Its **form** is a series of **logical steps** explaining why something is the case. For example, the first sentence makes a statement about Elvis's huge importance.
>
> - It uses **causal language**, for example, 'Elvis is called the King because he was the flashpoint… of a musical and cultural revolution.'
>
> - It contains a mixture of **present** and **past tense**, depending on the focus, for example, 'Elvis is called the King' – present tense; 'Elvis Presley made musical and social history' – past tense.
>
> - It uses mainly **formal language**, for example, 'the most significant worldwide cultural phenomenon of the 20th century.'
>
> - It uses **colourful language** to entertain the reader, for example, 'the flashpoint', 'the linchpin', 'the centrepiece'.

1 Draw up a bulleted list of the main points that this passage makes.

2 a) What point does the author make in the first sentence of paragraph 3? What point is made in the second sentence?

  b) What is the link between these two sentences? What connective does the author use to make this link clear?

3 In paragraph 5, identify which verbs are in the present tense and which in the past tense. Explain why both tenses have been used.

4 'And, subsequently, something highly improbable happened to Elvis' (lines 28–29). Reword this formal statement using informal language.

5 Choose four examples of colourful language in this text, and explain what makes them effective.

Purpose

6 In pairs, discuss what the main purpose of this text is. Then write your answer in one or two sentences. Give reasons for your answer, using causal language.

Reading for meaning

7 'Elvis started out as a pretender to the throne and became the King' (lines 14–15). What does the author mean by this?

8 Elvis Presley 'will never die' (lines 57–58). Why not?

9 What is the purpose of the sidebars ('The King and I')? Are they effective?

Dashes are used in two main ways in the text

- **one dash** can extend a sentence – like this
- **two dashes** can interrupt a sentence – like this – before carrying on.

10 a) Find two examples of each type of dash in the text.

b) How could the author have punctuated these sentences differently?

11 The author ends with two very short paragraphs. Why does he do this, and what is the effect?

12 a) How does the author compare Elvis with The Beatles (paragraph 4)? Draw up a table to show their similarities and differences.

b) Why does the author compare Elvis and The Beatles?

Exploring further

13 Assess this text in pairs. Discuss whether it is a good explanation of why Elvis is so popular and important. Give your reasons, using causal language.

Focus on: An entertaining style

The author uses a rich vocabulary and an exciting style. The result is a text that entertains as well as explains. In this section we will look at some of the author's techniques.

Powerful words

The author uses interesting words where possible. This ensures that his writing is never dull.

Wr7 14 Which of the words in the box are nearest in meaning to the following?

a) grandiose

b) improbable

c) flawed

d) uncanny

> unbelievable   imperfect   fantastic   unlikely
> weak   strange   big-headed   inconsistent
> creepy   extraordinary   exaggerated

Powerful phrases

Sometimes two words can work together to make a powerful phrase:

'sneeringly sexy'
- links the adjectives 'sneering' and 'sexy' by making one of them into an adverb – 'sneeringly' instead of 'sneering'
- the alliteration of 's' adds impact

'vibrant and vulnerable'
- two words describing very different characteristics – bringing them together is unusual and powerful
- the alliteration of 'v' adds impact

15 Choose two pairs of words from the list below to make two effective phrases describing someone. It may help to turn some of the adjectives into adverbs. Explain why your phrases are effective.

> crazy   casual   close   chaotic   controlled   controversial   clinging   careful

Snappy sentences

The author sometimes uses very short sentences for effect – for example, 'Elvis Presley started the revolution' (lines 5–6).

16 a) Find three other short sentences in the passage. Explain what makes them effective.

b) 'Everyone' (line 26).
'The father of a generation's music' (line 52).
What is unusual about these sentences?

Lengthy lists

Sometimes piling example on example can also be effective.

17 Explain why the author has included the following lengthy lists. What effect do they have on the explanation in each case?

a) 'Elvis's image is on clocks, calendars, mugs, stamps, plates, toys, you name it' (lines 49–50).

b) '…innocent and calculating, vibrant and vulnerable, powerful and flawed – envied and admired…' (lines 54–56).

Influential voices

Key Writing

Wr10

18 a) Discuss with a partner who you think is the best singer or band today. Try to give reasons for your choice.

b) Then each write some notes on your chosen singer or band. Use some of the ideas that came up in your discussion.

c) Use these notes to draft two paragraphs of explanation, suitable for a school magazine. The heading is: 'Why _____ is the best'.

Decide how you will organise and link your paragraphs.

- Start by giving the reader some basic information about your singer.
- Give at least four reasons why they are the best at what they do. Remember to use causal language.
- Use powerful words and phrases, and snappy sentences in effective places.
- Include lists of examples to support some of your reasons.
- Check the formality of your explanation. Does it suit the audience?

Exploring further

19 Add some sidebars with quotes from real or made-up people. Put these in the text where they will help to support your explanation.

② God bless Africa!

Aims

- Read two very different maiden speeches by politicians
- Analyse the use of rhetorical devices in speech (R12)
- Use standard English to present your findings to the class (S&L2)

Nelson Mandela was released from prison in 1990. This is the final part of the speech that he gave in 1994, when he was sworn in as the first black president of South Africa.

The time for the healing of the wounds has come. The moment to bridge the chasms that divide us has come. The time to build is upon us. We have, at last, achieved our political emancipation. We pledge ourselves to liberate all our people from the continuing bondage of poverty, deprivation, suffering, gender and other discrimination.

We succeeded in taking our last steps to freedom in conditions of relative peace. We commit ourselves to the construction of a complete, just and lasting peace. We have triumphed in the effort to implant hope in the breasts of the millions of our people. We enter into a covenant that we shall build the society in which all South Africans, both black and white, will be able to walk tall, without any fear in their hearts, assured of their inalienable right to human dignity – a rainbow nation at peace with itself and the world.

…We dedicate this day to all the heroes and heroines in this country and the rest of the world who sacrificed in many ways and surrendered their lives so that we could be free. Their dreams have become reality. Freedom is their reward.

We are both humbled and elevated by the honour and privilege that you, the people of South Africa, have bestowed on us, as the first President of a united, democratic, non-racial and non-sexist government. We understand it still that there is no easy road to freedom. We know it well that none of us acting alone can achieve success. We must therefore act together as a united people, for national reconciliation, for nation building, for the birth of a new world.

25 Let there be justice for all. Let there be peace for all. Let there be work, bread, water and salt for all. Let each know that for each the body, the mind and the soul have been freed to fulfil themselves. Never, never and never again shall it be that this beautiful land will again experience the oppression of one by another and suffer the indignity of
30 being the skunk of the world. Let freedom reign. The sun shall never set on so glorious a human achievement!
God bless Africa!

This is Private Eye's version of Lord Kinnock's first speech in the House of Lords.

That Kinnock Maiden Speech in Full

Lord Kinnochio of Windbag: My Lords, Ladies and Lords. Pray silence for myself. And let me begin by totally and utterly refuting the claims which have been in the Tory press that I have at any time sought in any manner, shape or form to abolish Your Lordships' chamber, which is a total and utter lie, as is any suggestion that I ever described Your Lordships as a 'bunch of clapped-out geriatric spongers who should all be strung up'. Because what I totally and utterly said was that my admiration for this noble and ancient house was 'utterly total and totally utter'. And furthermore that throughout my long and distinguished life in public service my constant and unwavering dream has been that one day I should be privileged to take my seat in this historic chamber, redolent as it is of the rich tapestry which has bound these island peoples together for centuries past. And today I say to you, this is not the end of my maiden speech. It is not even the end of the beginning. But it is the beginning of the end of the beginning which I must…

All Noble Lords: Shut up, you old windbag, get back to Brussels. Some of us are trying to get some sleep.

Key Reading

Persuasion texts

Nelson Mandela's speech is a **persuasion** text. Its **purpose** is to win the audience over to the speaker's message. The *Private Eye* **parody** of Kinnock's speech is a spoof persuasion text.

The main features of Mandela's speech are:

- It presents a **single viewpoint** supported by a **series of points**. For example, Mandela begins by making the point that this is a critical time.
- It uses **emotive language**, for example, 'Let there be *peace* for all.'
- It uses **powerful imagery** to draw a picture in the audience's mind, for example, 'a *rainbow* nation at peace with itself and the world'.
- It uses **rhetorical techniques** to help get the message across, for example, '*Never, never* and *never* again.'

1. Summarise the points that Mandela makes in this speech. Try to come up with one or two sentences summarising each paragraph.

2. Mandela uses some simple but emotive words, such as 'peace', which have a lot of meaning and feeling behind them. Find four highly emotive words in the speech and explain your choice.

3. The speech includes two striking images – South Africa, once 'the skunk of the world' (line 31), is now to be 'a rainbow nation' (line 13). Explain what makes these images effective.

4. **a)** What rhetorical technique does 'never, never and never again' use?

   b) How would Mandela have delivered these words for maximum impact?

> **rhetorical techniques** used to persuade an audience – for example, sound effects, exaggeration or repetition

God bless Africa!

Purpose

5 In this speech, President Mandela looks back over the past, assesses the present, and gives his audience a vision of the future of South Africa.

a) In groups, draw up a table like the one below.

References to: **The past**	**The present**	**The future**
achieved emancipation (line 3)	it's time to heal wounds (line 1)	we will free everyone from poverty, etc. (lines 4–5)

b) Does the past, the present or the future dominate? Why?

c) Identify the key words or phrases in Mandela's vision of the future.

6 What is the main purpose of the *Private Eye* column? How does this contrast with that of Mandela's speech?

Reading for meaning

7 a) Point to three features that make Mandela's speech formal.

b) Why is it written in such formal language?

8 The personal pronouns 'we', 'us' and 'our' are used over twenty times in Mandela's speech. They are a very formal version of 'I', 'me' and 'my', often used by monarchs and leaders to show that they represent the whole people. What is the overall effect of using so many of these pronouns in the speech?

9 In pairs, prepare a reading of Mandela's speech. Focus on:
- emphasising the key words
- pausing at key points
- varying the volume and pitch (high/low) of your delivery
- building up to a powerful ending.

Exploring further: Analysing humour

S7

10 Read the parody of Lord Kinnock's speech again. What makes it funny? Explore the following ideas in your answer, quoting examples:
- It presents Lord Kinnock as very self-important.
- It distorts rhetorical techniques to make the speech sound empty and dull.
- It presents politicians as deceitful.

Focus on: Rhetorical techniques

Here are seven rhetorical techniques used by President Mandela in his speech:

Repetition
Repeating the same word, phrase or sentence structure to hammer the point home. For example: 'Let there be justice for all. Let there be peace for all.'

Making a list
Listing different examples of the same thing emphasises the point and builds up momentum. For example: '…*the body, the mind and the soul* have been freed…'

Using personal pronouns
Using 'you' engages with the audience directly. Using 'I' or 'we' includes the audience on the speaker's side. For example, '*We* pledge *ourselves* to liberate all *our* people.'

Exaggeration
Overstating a view or a statistic to impress. For example: '…build the society in which all South Africans will be able to walk tall…'

Emotive language
Using words designed to stir the audience's feelings. For example: 'this beautiful land.'

Influential voices

Sound devices
Using sound effects, such as alliteration or rhyming, to make the point more attractive to the ear. For example: 'We *c*ommit ourselves to the *c*onstruction of a *c*omplete, just and lasting peace.'

Figurative language
Using strong images to help get the message across. For example: 'a rainbow nation.'

Archaic language
Using old-fashioned language and/or sentence structure. For example: 'We know it well that…'

R12

11 Look through Mandela's speech in pairs. Identify the rhetorical techniques he has used and discuss how effective they are. Draw up a table like the one below to record your findings.

Example	Rhetorical technique	Effect
Let there be justice for all. Let there be peace for all. (line 25)	repetition, sound effect	Very strong repetition – only one word different in each case. Puts the point across well.

Exploring further: Parodying rhetoric

12 Which of these rhetorical techniques are used in the parody of Lord Kinnock's maiden speech? Decide how the writer makes their effect humorous rather than persuasive.

Key Speaking and Listening

S&L2

13 Your task is to make a formal presentation to the class about the rhetorical techniques in President Mandela's speech. You can also refer to the way the *Private Eye* speech distorts rhetoric. Working in pairs, prepare to:

- Explain what rhetorical techniques are, and what they are for.
- Choose one or two examples of each rhetorical technique. Show how they work, and how effective they are in your view.
- Show how rhetorical techniques can be exaggerated or distorted for humorous effect. For example, repetition:

  In 'The time for the healing of wounds has come. The moment to bridge the chasms that divide us has come' the repetition of the sentence structure gives the opening a powerful rhythm. In the parody, 'totally' and 'utterly' are repeated too many times, and in silly variations, so that the effect is humorous rather than powerful.

- End your presentation with an assessment of the difference that delivery makes to the power of a persuasive text.
- Make your presentation in standard English. Imagine that this is a formal occasion – discuss with your partner how you can make your language and presentation as formal as possible.

Exploring further

14 Listen to the presentations of other pairs. Jot down some notes on how effective their **delivery** (their style of public speaking) is. Have any rhetorical techniques been used? Make one suggestion to each pair as to how to improve their delivery.

15 Try to write a parody of the opening paragraph of Mandela's speech. Exaggerate and distort the rhetorical techniques, such as repetition, emotive language and listing already present, and refer back to the *Private Eye* speech for ideas.

Influential voices

3 Writing to a celeb

Aims

- Read some advice for young people on how to get a celeb to help with your campaign
- Evaluate the presentational devices used in the text (Wr4)
- Write and present the next section of advice (Wr15)

The following is part of a 'campaigning toolkit' website for young people.

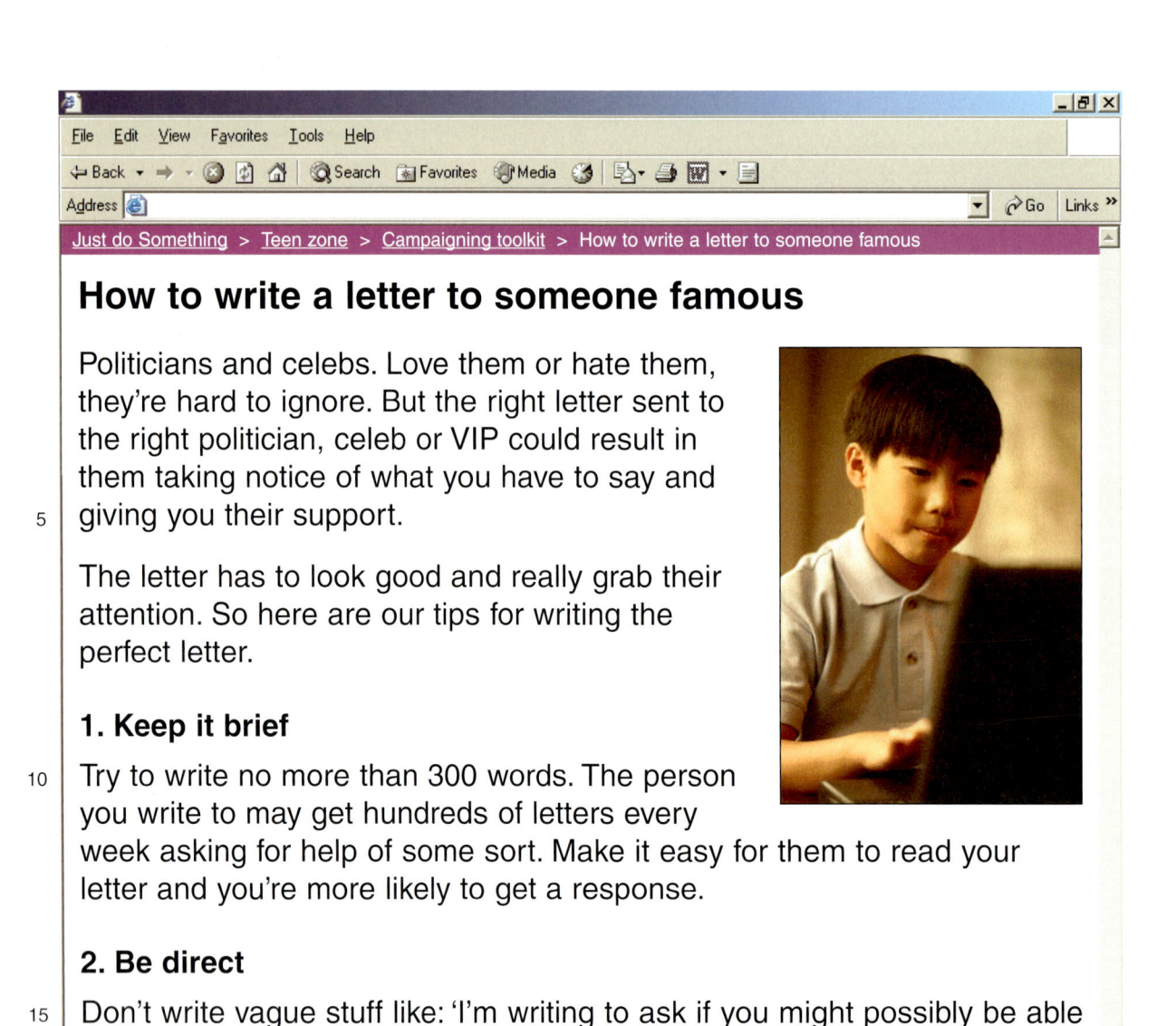

Just do Something > Teen zone > Campaigning toolkit > How to write a letter to someone famous

How to write a letter to someone famous

Politicians and celebs. Love them or hate them, they're hard to ignore. But the right letter sent to the right politician, celeb or VIP could result in them taking notice of what you have to say and
5   giving you their support.

The letter has to look good and really grab their attention. So here are our tips for writing the perfect letter.

1. Keep it brief

10   Try to write no more than 300 words. The person you write to may get hundreds of letters every week asking for help of some sort. Make it easy for them to read your letter and you're more likely to get a response.

2. Be direct

15   Don't write vague stuff like: 'I'm writing to ask if you might possibly be able to help out with a project I am working on' – this tells nobody anything.

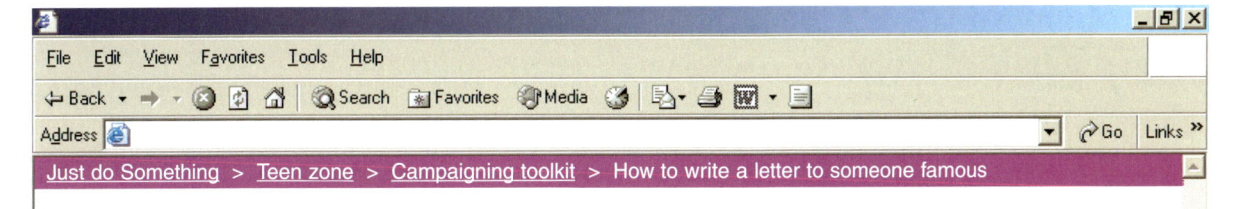

Just do Something > Teen zone > Campaigning toolkit > How to write a letter to someone famous

3. Get to the point – fast!

For example: 'Young people in this area are about to lose their only local theatre club. I'm campaigning to stop that happening.'

4. Explain who you are

How are you connected with the issue? Why do you feel so strongly about it?

For example: 'I'm a member of a youth drama club with 85 members from this town all aged between 13 and 18. We put on five plays each year, and it's a real chance for us to meet up and do something fun.'

5. Give the facts

- What is the campaign about?
- Who does it affect?
- How will it improve things?
- What are you doing to make it happen?

For example: 'The youth theatre is closing because the council can't afford to mend the roof and make it safe. There is no other theatre within walking distance where we can all meet, so the youth drama club will have to close too. We want to raise £8,000 to pay for the work and keep the theatre open.'

6. Say what you want

You need to tell them what you want them to do – whether it's making a personal appearance or asking a question in parliament. Spell it out.

You could write something like: 'We are putting on a comedy in the park this June to raise money. Would you be willing to come on stage for 10 minutes before the show to explain what we're doing to raise money and why?'

What Michelle did

Michelle sent a letter to her local MP complaining about the state of the area she lives in, which she says doesn't have its own hospital, cinema or any decent places to go.

'I showed the letter I was going to send to my mum. She checked it out for me because I'm terrible at spelling. She said it was fine but that I was a bit abrupt. So I made it a bit tamer. If I received a letter and it was really rude, I know I wouldn't do anything about it.

'My dad's reaction was like, "If you think you're going to get somewhere with this, you've got another think coming." When I got a letter back replying to mine, he was like, "Oh my God!" He was so surprised.'

Writing to a celeb

Influential voices

Key Reading

Advice texts

This is an **advice** text. Its **purpose** is to give advice and persuade the reader to take it.

The main features of this text are:

- It presents a **series of points**, often made easy to read by **presentational devices**. For example, the main points have numbered headings.
- It gives **examples** of how to write the letter, for example, 'I am a member of a youth drama club…'
- It uses **direct address** to speak to the reader, for example, 'Try to write no more than 300 words.'
- It uses a **conversational, informal tone** to get on the reader's side, for example, '*Don't* write vague *stuff* like…'
- It features an **opening** to hook the reader, for example, 'Politicians and celebs. Love them or hate them…'

1 The first part of this text has been annotated below to bring out some of the key features of advice texts. Make notes on lines 9–28 (up to the end of section 4) in the same way. Then comment on the effect of each feature.

---

informal language: contraction

purpose of text given clearly in heading

How to write a letter to someone famous

Politicians and celebs. Love them or hate them, they're hard to ignore. But the right letter sent to the right politician, celeb or VIP could result in them taking notice of what you have to say and giving you their support.

strong opening to hook reader

direct address

first clear point made

informal language: colloquialism

2 What presentational devices are used on this webpage? Are they effective?

3 Find one example of how to write to a celeb, and one example of how *not* to write to a celeb in this advice.

4 How does the writer address the reader in this extract?

5 Find three examples of the writer's conversational tone and explain why an informal tone has been used.

Purpose

6 The purpose of the webpage is given in its title. But what is the exact purpose of:

a) the first eight lines before the numbered points begin

b) the side panel 'What Michelle did'?

Reading for meaning

7 The text begins with the sentence 'Politicians and celebs.'

a) What is special about this sentence?

b) How else could the writer have punctuated the first two sentences?

c) Which is the better way, in your opinion?

8 Michelle's quote is even more informal than the rest of the writing on the webpage.

a) Give two examples of colloquial language used by Michelle.

colloquial the language used in conversation

b) Rewrite these examples in formal language.

9 How good are the writer's own examples of how to write? Analyse the examples under sections 4 and 5 by comparing them against the advice in the relevant section.

10 This advice includes imperatives (commands), for example: 'Get to the point' (line 17). But it also tries to 'soften' its commands in places, for example: 'Try to write…'(line 10).

   a) Find two other examples of a 'softened' command.

   b) Why has the author used these as well as straight imperatives?

11 This text includes only the first six sections of advice. There are four more. Discuss with a partner what other pieces of advice a young campaigner would like to have about writing a letter to a celeb. Select the four that you would include.

> ## Exploring further: Affect and effect
>
> Section 5 of the webpage includes the sentence 'Who does it affect?' (line 31). People often confuse the words 'affect' and 'effect'.
>
> - **Effect** is usually a noun – it means the result that someone or something has, or the overall impression of something.
> - **Affect** is usually a verb – it means to influence or have an effect on something or something.
>
> **12** Write two sentences to show that you understand the correct use of each word.

Focus on: Presentational devices

Wr4

13 How you present your advice visually is also important. In pairs, discuss the visual presentation of the campaign webpage. Draw up an evaluation table like the one below. Be prepared to present this to the class.

Presentational device	Good points	How to improve
font(s) used	same font used – very clear	could have different font in the 'Michelle' sidebar for variety

Think about the use of these features:
- colour
- bullet points and headings
- space/overall design
- image used
- website features such as navigation bars.

14 Imagine that you were designing a leaflet rather than a webpage for this advice. Would you change any of these features? If so, how? And for what reasons?

Exploring further: Using bullet points

When you write bullet points, each point must follow on grammatically from the opening statement. For example:

Make sure you:
- take regular exercise
- eat healthy food
- pamper yourself sometimes.

✓

Make sure you:
- take regular exercise
- healthy food is good for you
- you must pamper yourself as well.

✗

Bullet points also work best if they are roughly the same length, and are not too long.

15 Has the writer of the webpage followed this advice on bullet points?

Wr12

16 Write a short piece of advice on using bullet points. Make sure you use the bullet points correctly.

Key Writing

Wr15   **17** Write the section of the webpage that advises readers on how to check their campaign letter.

a) First, brainstorm what you want to say. Jot your main points down on the left-hand side of the paper. Add any supporting points or good words/phrases on the right, like this:

> type the letter on a computer — better than scribbling it in awful handwriting
> — good presentation is half the battle

You may want to cover some or all of these points:
- checking spelling/grammar
- checking that your main points are clear
- including name, address, contact numbers
- layout/presentation of letter
- keeping it brief.

b) Arrange your points in a logical order. This forms the plan for your section of advice.

c) On your own, use your plan to draft the section. Remind yourself of the key features of advice texts before you start.

d) Finally, write up your section and check it. Add a heading and effective presentational devices – these can be different from those used in the rest of the webpage, if you like.

Exploring further

18 Plan and write the final section of the webpage – 'Following up your letter'. Think about these issues:
- how long you wait after sending the letter
- making a phone call
- dealing with the celeb's secretary/PA (personal assistant).

④ Unit 3 Assignment: Mobiles for mums

Assessment Focus

▶ AF2 Produce texts appropriate to task, reader and purpose

> **You:** work in the advertising department of a mobile phone company.
>
> **Your task:** to write a leaflet persuading more adults to buy your range of mobile phones. You will need your skills in persuasive writing.

Stage 1

In pairs, discuss what form the leaflet will take:

- How much of it will be text, and how much image?
- What image(s) do you want to include, and why?
- What will be the overall tone of the leaflet? (Think about the audience.)

Stage 2

Now brainstorm some ideas for the text. Think how you could persuade older people that mobile phones are a good idea.

Jot down your main points on the left-hand side of a piece of paper. Add supporting points or good words/phrases on the right, like this:

useful for emergencies when travelling
— you may need to call the AA/emergency services
— tell your loved one you'll be late

Include at least five main points. For example:
- where/when a mobile is useful
- how easy it is to use
- how the expense can be kept down
- why mobiles make you feel in touch/younger.

Take the five best points from your brainstorm and list them in the most effective order. Add further key phrases or supporting points if they are missing.

Stage 3

Now write your leaflet. Remember:
- Use emotive language, for example:
  'Waiting at the roadside? Worried about a loved one?'
- Begin each paragraph with a topic sentence to make the point clear.
- Use direct address and personal pronouns to grab the reader/get them on your side.
- Include some rhetorical devices, such as repetition, sound effects, making a list or exaggeration.
- Vary the length of your sentences for effect.
- Think carefully about your tone. You are addressing older people, not teenagers. How formal should your language be?

Then add the final touches:
- Think of an attention-grabbing title.
- Give your paragraphs snappy subheadings.
- Add a 'quote' from a satisfied customer.

Challenge

- Think of a name for your phone company, and a good slogan. Add these to your leaflet.
- Think of a powerful image that will link your phones with a youth-giving image.
- Use ICT to design your leaflet.

Unit 4 Inside poetry

1 On the eighth day…

Aims

- Read the poem *On the eighth day…*
- Learn what parody and irony mean (S7)
- Identify the language used and the form of a poem
- Use a poem as a model to write your own (Wr8)

Read the following poem by Claire Calman. What does it remind you of?

On the eighth day…

In the beginning God created the heaven and the
    earth…
…and the computer.
And God said, Let there be light.
5   And the computer said: Sorry, a system error has
    occurred.
And God said, This is not what I had planned for the
    first day.
On the second day,
10 God said, let there be hardware and let there be
    software and let there be specialists, each who may
    comprehendeth one yet not the other.
And the computer said: This disk is incompatible.
On the third day,
15 God said, let there be disks of many diverse kinds, each
    yielding forth its own programme and let each

become redundant even on the same day it finally becomes affordable.

On the fourth day,

God said, Good grief, do I really have to wait till Sunday for the rest?

And the computer said: Please check connections and try again.

And God spent the fifth day listening to Richard Clayderman music while on hold for technical support.

On the sixth day,

God saw that there was not a man to till the ground and He said,

Let there be man to have dominion over the sea and the earth and – with any luck – over this computer.

And the Lord God breathed life

Into the microchips that lay scattered on the earth and, lo, there was…

Bill Gates.

On the seventh day,

God said, I really could do with a small nap.

On the eighth day,

The computer unplugged God and deleted Him from the system software.

Richard Clayderman a popular pianist

Key Reading

Poetry

This text is a **poem**. Its **purpose** is to explore feelings and ideas.

A poem is made up of **images**, **rhythm** and **form.**
- The **images** are the pictures made by the words.
- The **rhythm** is like the beat in music.
- The **form** is the framework or pattern of the poem. This can vary greatly.

A poem can be written:
- in any number of lines
- in a set number of lines that follow certain rules (for example, a sonnet)
- in verses (or stanzas)
- as a word picture (for example, a shape poem).

Poems can be written in different styles:
- Some poems **rhyme**.
- Some poems are **free verse**. They have lines of different lengths with different rhythms. (Some free verse contains rhyme.)

1 a) Sum up in two sentences what the poem is about.

  b) What is the significance of the conclusion?

2 What kind of humour would you say the poem uses?

3 Is the poem written in free verse or does it have a regular rhythm?

4 What gives the poem form?

5 Which two images from the poem most appeal to you? Give reasons for your choices.

Purpose

6 a) Why might the writer have written the poem? Think of several reasons.

b) What more serious point is being made about computers in this poem?

Reading for meaning

This poem is a **parody**, a type of comic poem in which the poet mimics the style of another writer or poem. This creates a comic effect, but the original must be a serious piece of writing for parody to work. The reader must also be able to recognise the poem's connection with the original text.

7 What is the original text on which the poem is based?

> ### Exploring further: Irony
>
> **Irony** occurs when something is said or happens that means the opposite of what was intended. It can also emphasise the difference between how things seem and how they really are.
>
> **8** Explain in two or three sentences why *On the eighth day…* is ironic. Read the first and last lines again and consider what else is mentioned, apart from God and the computer. How is the humour created?

Archaic language

As you may have deduced, the poem is written in the style of the Creation story from the *Book of Genesis* in the Bible. The writer uses several techniques to create humour.

- She uses **archaic** words and expressions (old-fashioned words and phrases that are no longer in use). For example, 'Let there be…' (Today we would say 'There will be…'.)
- A mock archaic style is used. Modern vocabulary is used alongside old-fashioned expressions, for example, 'Let there be specialists, each who may comprehendeth…'
- Phrases from everyday informal speech are also used, adding an informal **register**, for example 'I really could do with a small nap…'

9 In pairs, read through the poem and find two more examples of each of these techniques.

10 Try creating your own mock archaic phrases, using some of the language features of the following examples:

- 'I say unto you'
- 'So be it'
- 'And he spake thus'
- 'Thou doth mock me'

> **Grammar for reading**
>
> The **register** is the style of speech used in a particular situation and might be formal or informal.

Focus on: The conversation poem

This poem is also a conversation between God and the computer.

11 Discuss the following with a partner:

   a) What is the relationship like between the two?

   b) How is this similar to many people's relationships with their computers?

12 What is the difference in style between the way God speaks and the way the computer speaks? Does God use more than one style? Identify examples of words and expressions for each style and discuss the effect they create.

> **Exploring further: Technical terms**
>
> Technical expressions relating to IT are used in the poem when the computer speaks. Think about how this affects the nature of the computer's voice.
>
> **13** Using what you know of IT terminology, think of three other expressions that would suit the computer's voice, and write them down.

Repetition

14 In groups of three, read the poem aloud. Each take different parts (remember that there is also a commentary in the poem). Pay attention to the different language styles and tones of voice used.

Once you have read the poem aloud, you should be more aware of the repeating pattern in the poem. This gives the poem form.

15 a) Look through the poem again and find the repeating pattern.

b) Where is there a major change in the pattern? Why?

16 Now read the following. It is the first few lines of a poem by Christopher Smart (1722–1771) written in praise of his cat, in eighteenth-century English. Read the notes accompanying it.

Of Jeoffrey, His Cat

For I will consider my Cat Jeoffrey.
For he is the servant of the living God, duly and daily serving him.
For at the First glance of the glory of God in the East he worships in his way.
5   For this is done by wreathing his body seven times round with elegant quickness.
For then he leaps up to catch the musk, which is the blessing of God upon his prayer.
For he rolls upon prank to work it in.
10   For having done duty and received blessing he begins to consider himself.
For this he performs in ten degrees.
For first he looks upon his fore-paws to see if they are clean.
For secondly....

Repetition and listing give the poem form and help to create rhythm

Capital letters are used more freely

On the eighth day...

Exploring further

An **ode** is a poem written in praise of someone or something over several stanzas (verses). The language is elevated and the subject addressed directly as an ideal or symbol of perfection. For example, the following lines are from the poetry of John Keats (1795-1821):

- 'O latest born and love liest vision far…' (*Ode to Psyche*)
- 'Thou wast not born for death, immortal Bird!' (*Ode to a Nightingale*).

Key Writing

17 Your task is to write a poem complaining about or praising the latest IT device that interests you. For example, it might be the latest sound system, mobile phone or PC.

a) First choose a repeating pattern for your poem.

- If you write in complaint, you could refer to, *On the eighth day…* and start:
  'In the beginning God created heaven and earth… and… (add your IT device) On the first day…'

  Remember, this is a conversation poem, so try to bring out the difference in the voices involved.

- If you write in praise, you could start in the same way as *Of Jeoffrey, His Cat*:
  'For I will consider my…' (add your IT device)
  or you could use some of the features of an ode:
  'O thou beautiful source of musical entertainment…'

b) Once you have decided on your pattern, note down your main ideas. Try to use a mix of archaic and everyday language. Use your notes to produce a first draft.

c) Ask a partner to read your draft and find up to three ways in which it might be improved. Could the style of the voices contrast more? Could the archaic language sound more authentic? Does the humour in the complaint come through?

d) Redraft your poem on the computer using your partner's suggestions. Choose fonts to suit the style of your poem, including one to suit the archaic language you have used.

2 Two views on love

Aims

- Read two poems by different poets from different times
- Identify the themes of both poems
- Study the poetic techniques used
- Consider the form of each poem
- Compare the two poems (R17, Wr17)

The first poem is by Lord Byron (1788–1824). He belonged to a group of poets called the Romantics. They broke away from the kind of poetry being written in the late eighteenth century, which was more concerned with rational thought and balance. The Romantics were interested in emotions, the imagination, nature and freedom of expression.

When we two parted

When we two parted
In silence and tears,
Half-broken hearted,
To sever for years,
5   Pale grew thy cheek and cold,
Colder thy kiss,
Truly that hour foretold
Sorrow to this!

The dew of the morning
10 Sunk chill on my brow;
It felt like the warning
Of what I feel now.
Thy vows are all broken,
And light is thy fame:
15 I hear thy name spoken
And share in its shame.

They name thee before me,
A knell to mine ear;
A shudder comes oe'r me –
Why wert thou so dear?
They know not I knew thee
Who knew thee too well:
Long, long shall I rue thee
To deeply to tell.

In secret we met:
In silence I grieve
That thy heart could forget,
Thy spirit deceive.
If I should meet thee
After long years,
How should I greet thee? –
With silence and tears.

This poem by John Agard takes a different view of love, perhaps a wiser one.

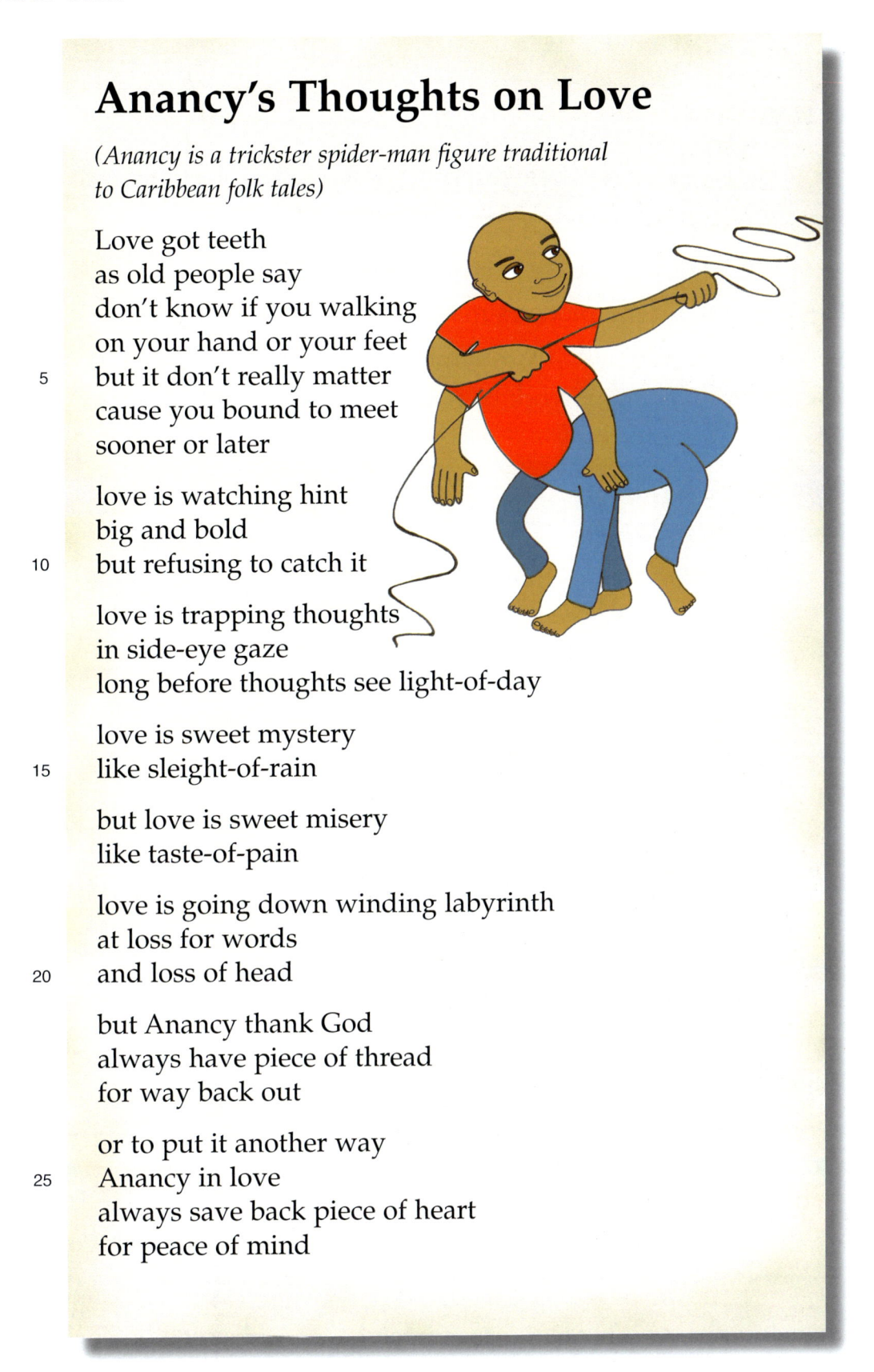

Anancy's Thoughts on Love

(Anancy is a trickster spider-man figure traditional to Caribbean folk tales)

Love got teeth
as old people say
don't know if you walking
on your hand or your feet
5   but it don't really matter
cause you bound to meet
sooner or later

love is watching hint
big and bold
10 but refusing to catch it

love is trapping thoughts
in side-eye gaze
long before thoughts see light-of-day

love is sweet mystery
15 like sleight-of-rain

but love is sweet misery
like taste-of-pain

love is going down winding labyrinth
at loss for words
20 and loss of head

but Anancy thank God
always have piece of thread
for way back out

or to put it another way
25 Anancy in love
always save back piece of heart
for peace of mind

Inside poetry

Key Reading

> ## Poetry
>
> These texts are **poems**. Their **purpose** is to explore feelings and ideas.
>
> A poem is made up of **images**, **rhythm** and **form**.
> - The **images** are the pictures made by the words.
> - The **rhythm** is like the beat in music.
> - The **form** is the framework or pattern of the poem. This can vary greatly.
>
> A poem can be written:
> - in any number of lines
> - in a set number of lines that follow certain rules (for example, a sonnet)
> - in verses (or stanzas)
> - as a word picture (for example, a shape poem).
>
> Poems can be written in different styles:
> - Some poems **rhyme**. Poems with regular rhyming patterns are said to have a **rhyme scheme**.
> - Some poems are **free verse**. They have lines of different lengths with different rhythms. (Some free verse contains rhyme.)

1 a) What aspects of love are expressed in both poems? Choose from the list below.

cautious love	rejected love	tragic love	true love
flippant love	despairing love	love's power	young love
passion	infatuation	an understanding of love	

b) Which of the remaining aspects are only expressed in one of the poems? List these separately under the poem titles.

c) Find words in each poem as evidence for your choices.

2 How would you describe the form of *Anancy's Thoughts on Love*?

3 Do the two poems have any features in common? If so, what?

4 Which image do you find most powerful in each poem? Why?

5 Think of a poem or rhyme that has a series of regular verses. What other features does it have?

Purpose

6 What do you think Byron's main purpose was when he wrote *When we two parted*? Refer to the information about the Romantics above the poem.

7 a) What do you think Anancy would feel about the emotions expressed in Byron's poem? Why?

b) Is *When we two parted* relevant to young people today? Why or why not? Think of more than one reason.

Reading for meaning

Byron's poem explores the emotions felt when a love affair is over. The **mood** is intense and dramatic. Repetition and alliteration are used for effect.

8 Identify examples of these techniques in the poem. In each case, how do these effects add to the meaning of the poem? What do they emphasise?

There are also mysteries and warnings in Byron's poem. The lover's name is never mentioned, and there is the suggestion of a secret.

9 a) In pairs, write out the lines below and discuss what they suggest and how they are ironic. (Check the meaning of 'irony' on page 75.)

> They know not I knew thee
> Who knew thee too well

b) Which other lines in the poem suggest a secret? What do you think the secret might be?

c) What are your main conclusions about why the affair ended?

The stanza

A **stanza** is another name for a verse. When we use the term 'stanza' we are referring to poems that have regular patterns. For example, a poem written in stanzas often has:

- the same number of lines in each verse
- the same pattern of rhyme or **rhyme scheme**.

10 What regular patterns exist in *When we two parted*?

The patterns in the poem may be regular and ordered, but in contrast the feelings involved are anything but ordered or controlled. By creating a regular pattern, the poet is trying to order and understand this mixture of feelings.

> ### Exploring further: A different perspective
>
> Some critics in the past were very opposed to the Romantics. T. E. Hulme saw Byron's poetry as the work of a fevered imagination 'which doesn't consider a poem is a poem unless it is moaning or whining about something or other'.
>
> **11** Is Byron only 'moaning and whining' in *When we two parted*?
>
> In a group, discuss reasons for and against this point of view, and make notes. Consider:
>
> - whether the feelings expressed are likely to be real or not (Does this matter?)
> - whether poets should concern themselves with some topics more than others (for example, world poverty rather than personal feelings).

Focus on: Another point of view

In *Anancy's Thoughts on Love* the poet uses a figure from Caribbean folk tales to explore love in a different way. Anancy has a cooler, more cautious attitude to love.

12 a) What does the word 'trapping' suggest about love in these lines?

> love is trapping thoughts
> in side-eye gaze

b) What is Anancy? What does love in the poem have in common with him? Refer back to the lines above.

13 a) What advice would Anancy give about love? Reread verses 7 and 8.

b) Anancy's advice could be viewed as wise or uncaring. In pairs, discuss other ways in which it can be viewed, in both a positive and a negative light.

Rhythm

14 In pairs, read *Anancy's Thoughts on Love* aloud and note down lines that feel particularly rhythmic.

Remember that although free verse does not have a regular rhythm, it does still have rhythm. Certain features enhance the rhythm, such as the use of compound words, which run together, emphasising their movement.

15 a) Find examples of these compound words in the poem.

b) What is the effect of each of these examples?

Exploring further: Language and style

16 Why is the language in John Agard's poem suited to the figure of Anancy? Identify particular words or images to support your answer.

Two views on love

Key Writing

R17, Wr17

17 a) Work with a partner to compare the two poems about love. First, draw up a table like the one below and use it record the similarities between the poems. Add lines from each poem as evidence to support your ideas, as shown in this example:

When we two parted / Anancy's Thoughts on Love		
Similarities	**Evidence:** When we two parted	**Evidence:** Anancy's Thoughts on Love
Both poems acknowledge that love can be painful	'When we two parted In silence and tears'	'but love is sweet misery like taste-of-pain'

b) Continue the table, focusing on the differences between the two poems. Keep your work for the assignment on pages 95–97.

Remember to include notes on these areas:
- the content and theme of the poems
- the form of the poems
- use of poetic techniques
- language choice.

Exploring further: Using quotation marks

When you write an analysis of a text you need to support what you say by referring to the text. Sometimes this needs a quotation. To take the example from the table above, we can include the quotation in the actual sentence:

> While Byron's poem focuses on the pain of rejected love, John Agard's poem also acknowledges that 'love is sweet misery/ like taste-of-pain'.

use single quotation marks

S4

18 Write a paragraph about the two poems and use brief quotations to support what you say.

3 A strange welcome

Aims

- Read two poems by the same poet
- Identify the themes of the poems
- Consider the issues in the poems (R16)
- Learn about the voice of a poem
- Compare the two poems

The following two poems come from the same volume of poetry, *Propa Propaganda*, by Benjamin Zephaniah. As you read them, think about the connections between the two poems as well as the poet's concerns.

Homeward Bound

That old man
Cut sugarcane in Jamaica
After he graduated from Sunday School,
Fed up with cutting cane
5   He came here for a better life.
He came here on a big ship
With big dreams
And two guineas,
He came here full of hope
10 With a great big smile,
He came here for the welcome
And the promise.
If his mother (bless her soul) could see him now
She would cry for her baby.

15 He don't understand political correctness
Give him the money and he's gone,
He did not study the oral tradition
Give him a stage and
He will explain.
20 He came here with his ambitions
And his Christianity,

She came here with a nursery qualification
And his Christianity,
Between them they produced six Rastafarians
Who called themselves Lost Africans.

When the old man puts on his old suit
He dances like a rude boy
His music is in his head,
Now he dreams of fresh sugar cane,
When the old man
Puts on his everyday face
He is only grinning and bearing,
He did forty years on the buses
And he never went to jail.

The old man
Was going home anyway,
All his Jamaica nights are in his head,
Fed up with the weather
He wants a better life,
All his English days he voted Labour
But he thinks that Labour didn't vote for him,
And now he only wants to see his saviour
Sweet Jamaica.

That old man
Shall die in Kensal Rise
he knows it,
You know it
But don't tell him.

Neighbours

I am a type you are supposed to fear
Black and foreign
Big and dreadlocks
An uneducated grass eater.

5   I talk in tongues
I chant at night
I appear anywhere,
I sleep with lions
And when the moon gets me
10 I am a Wailer.

I am moving in
Next door to you
So you can get to know me,
You will see my shadow
15 In the bathroom window,
My aromas will occupy
Your space,
Our ball will be in your court.
How will you feel?

20 You should feel good.
You have been chosen.

I am the type you are supposed to love
Dark and mysterious
Tall and natural
25 Thinking, tea total.
I talk in schools
I sing on TV
I am in the papers,
I keep cool cats

30 And when the sun is shining
I go Carnival.

Benjamin Zephaniah

Inside poetry

Key Reading

Poetry

These texts are **poems**. Their **purpose** is to explore feelings and ideas.

A poem is made up of **images, rhythm** and **form**.
- The **images** are the pictures made by the words.
- The **rhythm** is like the beat in music.
- The **form** is the framework or pattern of the poem. This can vary greatly.

A poem can be written:
- in any number of lines
- in a set number of lines that follow certain rules (for example, a sonnet)
- in verses (or stanzas)
- as a word picture (for example, a shape poem).

Poems can be written in different styles:
- Some poems **rhyme**. Poems with regular rhyming patterns are said to have a **rhyme scheme**.
- Some poems are **free verse**. They have lines of different lengths with different rhythms. (Some free verse contains rhyme.)

1 a) In *Neighbours*, how does the first line set the tone of the verse?

  b) What are the main images of the Rastafarian in the first verse?

2 a) Find three contrasting images of the old man in *Homeward Bound* that show his different moods.

  b) Identify a line that sums up his dominant mood.

  c) How do you think the old man appears to others? Give examples of the lines that provide you with clues.

Purpose

3 In *Homeward Bound*, Zephaniah explores feelings and ideas through the figure of the old man. What feelings were you left with at the end of the poem?

4 a) How do you think Zephaniah presents the Rastafarian in *Neighbours*?

b) Do you think the poet is being entirely serious? Why?

5 Why do you think the poet decided to write these two poems? What were his concerns?

Reading for meaning

Themes

The **theme** of a poem is the main idea that connects the images in the poem to give a deeper meaning. For example, a theme might be 'love' or 'death' or 'justice'. A poem may also have more than one theme. In *Homeward Bound* the old man is central to the theme, but it could be about anyone in his situation.

6 a) In pairs, study the verses closely and trace the old man's life. Where hints are given, discuss how he feels about his different experiences.

b) Now discuss the following:

> Although the old man has returned to Jamaica through his memories ('All his Jamaica nights are in his head'), he can never return physically.
>
> However, we could argue that there is another sense in which he can never return. What is it? Look closely at the poem.

c) Sum up your views of the main themes in *Homeward Bound*, referring to your discussion.

A strange welcome

Exploring further: The newcomer

7 If people are not to feel as the old man does, what kinds of experiences must they have when they move to another country or neighbourhood?

8 Imagine that you have just moved to a new place. How have you travelled? By air, sea, road? What time of year is it? What time of day? Where are you exactly – in a new home, a new school?

Write a short poem – just a few lines - about what you see and feel. Try to use a single image that sums up the experience – for example, a sense of freedom or disappointment.

Focus on: Using humour to make a point

In contrast to *Homeward Bound*, *Neighbours* is a serious poem told in a humorous way. It focuses on a Rastafarian and the kinds of prejudice he comes across. He is presented using two different **stereotypes**. The poet mocks these stereotypes and so creates the humour in the poem. In other words, he uses **satire**.

9 a) In pairs, reread verses 1, 2 and 3 and make notes under the heading 'Stereotype 1'. Then read verses 4, 5 and 6 again and make notes under the heading 'Stereotype 2'.

b) Look carefully for words that give you clues as to which stereotype is being presented. Add these to your notes. For example, Zephaniah uses a pun in the following lines:

> 'And when the moon gets me
> I am a Wailer.' (lines 9–10)

'Wailer' refers to Bob Marley's reggae band 'The Wailers'. How is the poet mocking the stereotype here?

c) Using your notes, decide together what the main theme of the poem is.

> **stereotype** is an overly simple, fixed view of someone or something, usually based on prejudice
>
> **satire** a way of mocking individuals or society to expose prejudice, hypocrisy or foolishness
>
> **pun** a word with a double meaning, used to make a joke

Exploring further: Who is speaking?

When poets write using the first person 'I' they are not necessarily writing about themselves. By using the first person they can step into another's shoes more easily and speak directly to the reader. However, we could say that *Neighbours* is a personal poem, that the poet was thinking of himself when he wrote it.

10 What lines in the poem suggest this? How?

11 a) This poem was published in 1996. Read the first three verses again. What is the poet suggesting the attitude was to Rastafarians at the time? Do you think:

- attitudes have changed since the poem was written
- attitudes vary depending on other factors (for example, someone's personal background or where they live)?

Discuss your ideas with a partner.

b) Write a paragraph, taking these points into account.

A strange welcome

Key Writing

12 In pairs, compare *Homeward Bound* and *Neighbours*.
- Look through the work you have done.
- Share and develop your ideas together.
- If it helps to organise your ideas, draw up a table headed 'Similarities and Differences', and record notes and evidence. (See page 86 for an example.)

13 Choose one of the following writing tasks:

a) Write an essay comparing the two poems.
- Write one or two paragraphs to compare the similarities between the poems. Use connectives such as 'similarly', 'also' and 'in addition to' to link your ideas.
- Write one or two paragraphs to contrast the differences between the poems. Use connectives such as 'alternatively' and 'by contrast'.
- Include lines from the poem to support what you say, using single quotation marks.
- Include a final paragraph summing up the issues you think were uppermost in Zephaniah's mind when he wrote these poems. Say which poem you like best and why.

b) Write an essay discussing these questions:

Do you think both characters feel betrayed or not? What similarities and differences are there between their experiences?
- Use appropriate connectives to link and contrast your points.
- Include lines from the poem to support what you say.
- Include a final paragraph summing up your ideas. Say which character is more effectively portrayed and why.

④ Unit 4 Assignment: The critic

Assessment Focuses

- AF2 Produce texts which are appropriate to task, teacher and purpose
- AF3 Organise and present whole texts effectively, sequencing and structuring information, ideas and events

> **You:** are a poetry critic.
>
> **Your task:** to write a discursive essay comparing two poems.
>
> You will need the work you did on the poems *When we two parted* by Lord Byron and *Anancy's Thoughts on Love* by John Agard on pages 79-86.

Stage 1

First, plan your essay.

Introduction

Open by stating what you are going to do. Name the poems, who wrote them and any other important details. Then make two general statements, briefly stating what the poems have in common and how they differ.

The main section

Now compare the two poems in greater detail.

- Remember, you will need to select which points to include, as you will not have space or time to cover every example.
- Structure your essay discursively. This means you should discuss the poems together, making one or two points about Poem 1, then about Poem 2, showing how it is similar or different. Carry on in this way until you have addressed all your points.

Conclusion

Briefly note how you will sum up the main features of each poem, drawing out the contrasts between the two.

Stage 2

Think about how to organise your discursive essay.

To write well you will need to organise your points into several paragraphs and link them effectively.

For example, when writing about the poems, use connectives:
- of comparison ('in the same way', 'similarly', 'not only', 'also')
- of contrast ('on the one hand', 'on the other hand', 'whereas', 'although', 'the former', 'the latter')
- to qualify a point ('however') or to add a point ('in addition').

Try to support your comments by quoting from the poem.

Use some of the quotes you collected in the table completed for question 17, page 86. Remember to use single quotation marks when you quote from a text.

Stage 3

Now write your draft essay, referring to your plan. When you have completed your draft, look through it to see what might be improved.

For example, does your writing show clearly how meaning and style are linked?

> In Byron's poem the words 'with silence and tears' from the second line are **repeated** in the last, reinforcing **the pain of lost love** expressed in Byron's poem.

the pain of lost love → meaning
repeated → style

Challenge

Look back at question 11, page 84, and T. E. Hulme's comment about Byron and the Romantics. Write two paragraphs opposing this and supporting the Romantic view. Refer to *When we two parted* to support your argument.

Use the following points to help you:
- the poem's theme and relevance to modern life (for example, the feelings expressed in many pop songs and ballads)
- the universal nature of love
- the importance of the emotions featured.

Unit 5 On the streets

1 Stone Cold

Aims

- Read the opening scenes of a play script about being homeless, and explore their dramatic impact (R14)
- Perform one of these scenes, focusing on conveying character, atmosphere and tension (S&L14)
- Write a critical evaluation of several performances (S&L15)

The following extract is from the opening to a play by Joe Standerline, based on the novel *Stone Cold* by Robert Swindells.

```
       Scene 1
       The street. A litter bin. A yellow spot comes
       up on Link. He looks bored. His clothes are
       scruffy and he looks dirty. He takes a good
 5     look at the audience, then speaks to them.

       LINK  Have you ever sat and watched people, really
             watched them? They're all in their own little
             world. Now and then they'll let you in, if
             they're feeling brave or if they think they
10           know you. But the rest of the time you might
             as well be invisible.

       A couple of passers-by walk straight in front
       of him. One drops a crisp packet at his feet.
             See what I mean.
15     Link picks up the crisp packet and looks to see
       if there's anything left inside. There isn't. He
       moves towards the litter bin. The lights fade.

       Scene 2
       Shelter's living room. There is an armchair,
20     small table, standard lamp and fireplace. A
       doorway leads from this room to the bathroom
```

and kitchen. There is a window with heavy, drawn curtains. A cat lies quietly in a basket in front of the fireplace. Above is hung a portrait of an old-looking soldier. **Shelter** enters with a bowl of tomato soup.

SHELTER (Thinking out loud) Haven?... Home...House...

He sits down, puts his soup on the table and picks up a dictaphone and starts to record.

Day One. Everything is ready. Practice mission executed successfully. Executed. (*Sniggers. There's a knock at the door;* **Shelter** *ignores it.*) Only complaint at present time is constant pestering from man upstairs. Have now verified code name and will shortly post mission statement to relevant body. Operation to be known as...

He stops the tape for a time to think. He ignores another knock at the door.

Hostel?... Shack?... Shed?...

Another knock, he is slightly riled.

Shelter! That's it. (*Recording it.*) 'Operation Shelter!' Perfect. Succinct yet welcoming.

Switches the tape off and slurps a mouthful of soup. There's another knock, the soup drips from his mouth as he speaks.

Get. Lost.

He sits at the table and starts to write. Lights snap back to the street scene.

Scene 3

The street.

LINK Wish I *had* been invisible this afternoon though.

Mr Greenwood *appears in a spotlight. He peers forward, as if looking at Link.*

Mr Greenwood, my old geography teacher. Last time he saw me was in school, picking up my GCSE certificates. That was a couple of months ago now. Today, I was picking a half eaten bag of chips out of a rubbish bin...

65	**LINK**	*(Puts the crisp packet in the bin.)* He just stared at me at first. I wanted the ground to swallow me up. He started to make his way over.
	MR GREENWOOD	Are you who I think you are?
	LINK	I tried to ignore him. I twisted my face up a bit hoping he'd mistake me for a stranger.
70	**MR GREENWOOD**	David?
	LINK	*(Facing forward, as if talking to Mr Greenwood.)* You've got the wrong bloke mate sorry.

Key Reading

Play scripts

This text is a **play script**. Its **purpose** is to provide a written version of the play for the actors, director and anyone else developing play.

The main features of this text are:

- Its **layout** includes text divided into scenes and the names of characters on the left, in capitals. The characters' speech follows their names.
- It presents **visual information/directions** in italics. These can describe a scene or a character's actions, for example, *'A couple of passers-by walk straight in front of him.'*
- It contains **dialogue/speech** which is not presented in inverted commas, for example: '**SHELTER** Haven?… Home… House…'
- It uses **monologues** (speeches made directly to the audience) to let the audience know what is going on in the character's head, for example, '**LINK** Have you ever sat and watched people, really watched them?'
- There is a **build-up of tension** – we want to know what will happen, for example, why someone is knocking at Shelter's door.

1. Describe in one or two sentences what happens in Scene 1. Then do the same for Scene 2. Refer to the character and settings of each scene in your answer.

2. Find two stage directions in each scene. One of these should be a direction telling the actor how to say his lines.

3. a) Link and Shelter are alone in their scenes. What reason does the writer give each of them to speak?

   b) Are these methods realistic or effective?

4. Why do you think the author makes Link speak in such a straightforward way?

5. a) How is tension built up at the beginning of Scene 3?

   b) Predict how you think the scene will continue.

Purpose

6. A play script provides more information than just the actors' lines. What does this extract tell you about:

   a) the lighting effects

   b) the stage scenery

   c) the way the characters say their lines?

7. Scene 1 is very short, and not much happens. So why did Joe Standerline start his play with it? Find evidence in Scene 1 to support your choice.

Reading for meaning

8. Which word best describes the tone of Link's speech in Scene 1?

   ● thoughtful   ● angry   ● bored   ● resigned

   In pairs, take turns saying the lines in these different ways. Which seems most effective?

9. Much more detail about the setting is given in the stage directions for Scene 2. It is as if the writer wants to contrast the two settings. How could you bring out this contrast in an actual production?

On the streets

10 In the novel by Robert Swindells, the chapters are narrated alternately by Link and Shelter. This creates the effect of a dual 'voice'. How could a director play with this idea in the theatre? Discuss these possibilities:
- The scenes are acted at the same time, using voice overs.
- The actors are on the stage at all times, but the lighting picks them out in turn.

11 What do you think Operation Shelter is? What is the effect of leaving the audience in the dark about this?

Exploring further: Link's two roles

12 Link is both a narrator (addressing the audience) and a character. He mixes the two roles in Scene 3. How could a director make the separate roles clear?

Focus on: Conveying atmosphere, character and tension

13 Your task is to direct and perform Scenes 1 and 2, bringing out the different atmospheres, characters and tension of the scenes.

Link is described in the cast list as '16 years old'.

Shelter is described in the cast list as 'In his early forties; one serious headcase; thrown out of the army for being out of control'.

a) In groups of three, discuss the following questions:
- How could you present each character effectively? Consider:
  - their manner
  - their looks/dress
  - the way they deliver their lines.
- How could you make Scene 1 an effective opening to the play?
- How might you link Scenes 1 and 2 and with what effect?
- Does Shelter appear threatening straight away? Or does this happen gradually through the scene? How could you present this?
- How can the knocking on the door – and Shelter's reaction to it – be used to build up tension in the scene?

b) Make notes on a copy of Scenes 1 and 2 to bring out exactly how you would play it. Refer to the annotated example on the following page to help you.

> *Shelter enters with a bowl of tomato soup.*
>
> **SHELTER** *(Thinking out loud)* Haven?... Home... House...
>
> *He sits down, puts his soup on the table and picks up a dictaphone and starts to record.*

- Slightly irritated at not coming up with right name
- Don't slump – do everything crisply
- Come in briskly
- Leave good pauses between words

c) Still in groups, one of you takes the role of director and the other two the actors playing Link and Shelter. Rehearse each scene, making changes to your notes if necessary.

Key Speaking and Listening

14 a) Now join up with three other groups. Each group performs Scenes 1 and 2. Meanwhile the other groups make notes on the performances. Draw up a table like the one below, and record your thoughts:

	Group 1	Group 2	Group 3	Group 4
Acting – Do the characters: ● engage our attention? ● present a convincing character? ● develop through the scene?				
Directing – Is there: ● a sense of purpose and direction to the scene? ● a build-up of tension? ● any unusual interpretation? With what effect? ● effective linking between the two scenes?				

interpretation a particular approach to a performance, which makes that performance different from others

b) Write one paragraph on each performance, using the first person and the past tense. In each case, comment on two things that worked well, and one that could be improved.

On the streets

2 Killing with kindness

Aims

- Read a poster and webpage produced by a homelessness charity
- Explore how they present a persuasive case
- Present a more biased case, and analyse the bias used by others (Wr13, S&L6)

The poster below and webpage on pages 105–106 are both part of a campaign by Thames Reach Bondway, a homelessness charity.

**Can you spare 20p for a cup of tea?
How about £10 for a bag of heroin?
Or £12 for a rock of crack?**

The money you give to those who beg may help keep them on the streets. It may even help to buy the drugs that kill them. Put your spare change where it counts instead. Thames Reach Bondway – Ending street homelessness.

Killing with Kindness

Why Thames Reach Bondway believe giving to those who beg does more harm than good.

> 'Don't be mean, you heard the man, he wants a few pence for a cup of tea…'

The overwhelming evidence shows that people who beg on the street do so in order to buy hard drugs – particularly crack cocaine and heroin. These Class A drugs are highly addictive and eventually lead to extreme deterioration in health and even death.

Drug testing of people arrested for begging in Westminster disclosed that 77% of those arrested tested positive for Class A drugs.

> 'Maybe, but there's surely no harm in giving a few pence…'

Giving to people who beg is not a benign act without consequences. As an organisation that has worked with people on the street for over twenty years, we have seen many lives damaged by hard drugs and alcohol misuse. People have also died through overdoses. A significant portion of their income that was spent on drugs came from members of the public giving loose change.

> 'Come on, these are just people a bit down on their luck.'

During an exercise carried out in Westminster in partnership with the Metropolitan Police between April 2003 and March 2004 it was discovered that there was a hardcore group of 18 people who had been arrested on 299 occasions during the period for begging. Clearly these are not individuals in temporary difficulties but people who are dependent on a begging income. Almost certainly it will be to fund a serious drug habit.

> 'OK, you've convinced me. So how can I help people to get off the street and away from the dealers?'

On the streets

30 Here are some recommended alternatives to handing out 'spare change':
- You can buy the person a cup of tea or sandwich instead.
- You can spend time listening to them and finding out more about their needs.
35
- You can donate to a charity working with homeless people who can guarantee (and if necessary provide evidence) that your money is going directly to homeless people. Thames Reach Bondway is able to do so.
- You can volunteer to work with a homelessness agency such as
40 Thames Reach Bondway. To find out more, contact Tara Butler on 020 7702 5647 or via our website, www.thamesreachbondway.com.

Help Thames Reach Bondway to end street homelessness.

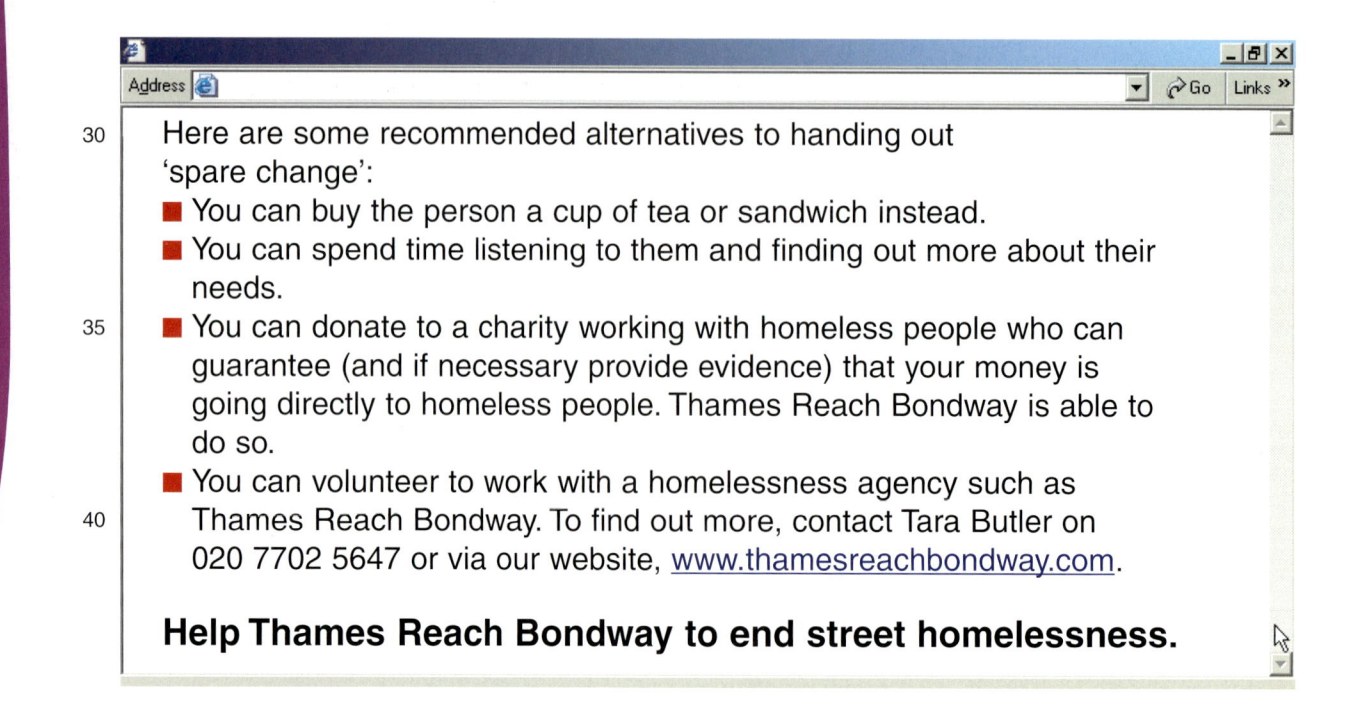

Key Reading

Persuasion texts

These texts are part of a series of **campaign material**. Their **purpose** is to persuade people not to give to beggars.

The main features of the poster are:
- It uses **visual images** to grab the interest of the reader and make an impact, for example, the figure made up of coins.
- It uses **emotive language**, for example, 'It may even help to buy the drugs that kill them…'

The main features of the webpage are:
- It uses **formal language**, for example, 'Clearly these are not individuals in temporary difficulties…'
- It includes **evidence** or **reasons** given for the points made, for example, 'The overwhelming evidence shows that…'
- It adopts a **reasonable tone**, for example, 'Almost certainly it will be to fund a serious drug habit.'

1. Analyse the visual impact of the poster. Consider the message sent by:
   a) the main image
   b) the style of the text
   c) the overall design.

2. How does the text on the poster draw you in to read further?

3. 'Put your spare change where it counts instead.'
   a) Why is this an effective sentence?
   b) Where *are* you being asked to put your spare change?

4. a) Identify two examples of formal language from the webpage, and two examples of informal language.
   b) Why have two different registers been used? Is this effective?

5. The main argument in the webpage is that giving to those who beg does more harm than good. Find three reasons to back this up.

register the level of formality of a text. Colloquial text is in a different register from a formal letter.

Purpose

6. Are the purposes of the poster and the webpage exactly the same? How does the purpose relate to the audience in each case? Discuss these questions in pairs. Find evidence in the texts to support your answers.

Reading for meaning

7. Explain the term 'direct address', using examples from the text on the poster. How effective is its use here?

8. Two London councils have adapted Thames Reach Bondway's campaign. Their poster has the same image of the coin figure, but the text above is:

> **Your kindness could kill**
> The money you give to those who beg may actually keep them on the streets.
> In some cases, you may even be helping them to buy drugs that could kill them.
> Give responsibly – support local charities instead.
> Please visit: www.killingwithkindness.com for more information.

Compare the two posters. Which is more effective at getting its message across? Give your reasons.

9 What other image could you use on a poster for this campaign?

    a) Think of one or two images of your own.

    b) Compare them with the coin figure.

10 The webpage uses a 'question and answer' format.

    a) Why has it been written like this?

    b) How effective is it?

11 The final section of the webpage is written and organised in a different way from the rest. Explain what purpose this has and identify two features as evidence for this.

12 The name 'Thames Reach Bondway' results from the merging of two homelessness organisations – Thames Reach and Bondway. Either:

- Explain why this is a good name for the new charity, or
- Think of an alternative name that is more effective.

Focus on: Making a persuasive case

The Thames Reach Bondway webpage makes its case by presenting a reasoned argument with a 'passer-by'. These are the methods used:

- formal language
- restrained tone
- giving evidence and facts
- impersonal language.

13 Identify two examples of each of these features in the first two sections of text.

The charity could have chosen a more **biased** way of presenting its case. Features of biased texts often include:

- emotive and rhetorical language, for example, 'killer drugs'
- giving opinions rather than facts, for example, 'It is disgraceful that…'
- using the first and second person to get the audience on side, for example, 'You must not give money'
- stereotyping people, for example, presenting all beggars as dangerous drug addicts to be avoided.

> **biased** unfairly presented to favour one point of view over another

A biased version of the first section could look like this:

second person – direct address

opinion given, with no evidence

stereotyping all beggars

emotive language

> You know that beggars are only on the street to fund their disgusting habit – hard drugs. And we're not talking about the odd spliff – we're talking crack cocaine and heroin. Their deadly cargo is addiction, decay and death.

emotive language

rhetorical effect of list of three, and alliteration of 'd' sound

first person – 'we' makes it more personal

Wr13

14 Rewrite Sections 2 and 3 of the text in a similar way. Use the techniques listed above to make your text as biased as possible.

15 Which is the more effective text for this purpose?

Exploring further: Context and audience

16 Where are you more likely to find the biased type of text?

17 How does its attitude to people who beg differ from the Thames Reach Bondway text?

On the streets

Key Speaking and Listening

S&L6

18 Join up with three other students. Then listen carefully as each reads out their text from question 14, and note down examples of bias. Draw up a table like the one below, using it to record how all four techniques of biased writing are used.

Examples of:	Student 1	Student 2	Student 3	Student 4
emotive and rhetorical language				
opinions rather than facts				
first and second person				
stereotyping				

Make sure you include an analysis of your own text.

19 Decide as a group:
- Which is the most biased text?
- Which is the most effective at biasing the audience?

3 London road

Aims

- Read an account of how a famous writer left home
- Explore how different tenses are used to describe events in the past
- Use reading and dramatic skills to explore the ideas and meaning of the passage (S&L12)
- Write about style, giving evidence from the text (Wr17)

In *As I Walked Out One Midsummer Morning*, Laurie Lee describes how he eventually left his family and home in the Cotswold countryside.

The stooping figure of my mother, waist deep in the grass and caught there like a piece of sheep's wool, was the last I saw of my country home as I left it to discover the world. She stood old and bent at the top of the bank, silently watching me go, one gnarled red hand raised in farewell and blessing, not questioning why I went. At the bend of the road I looked back again and saw the gold light die behind her; then I turned the corner, passed the village school, and closed that part of my life for ever.

It was a bright Sunday morning in early June, the right time to be leaving home. My three sisters and a brother had already gone before me; two other brothers had yet to make up their minds. They were still sleeping that morning, but my mother had got up early and cooked me a heavy breakfast, had stood wordlessly while I ate it, her hand on my chair, and had then helped me pack my few belongings. There had been no fuss, no appeals, no attempts at advice or persuasion, only a long and searching look. Then, with my bags on my back, I'd gone out into the early sunshine and climbed through the long wet grass to the road.

It was 1934. I was nineteen years old, still soft at the edges, but with a confident belief in good fortune. I carried a small rolled-up tent, a violin in a blanket, a change of clothes, a tin of treacle biscuits, and some cheese. I was excited, vain-glorious, knowing I had far to go; but not, as yet, how far. As I left home that morning and walked away from the sleeping village, it never occurred to me that others had done this before me.

I was propelled, of course, by the traditional forces that had sent many generations along this road – by the small tight valley closing in around one, stifling the breath with its mossy mouth, the cottage walls narrowing like the arms of an iron maiden, the local girls whispering, 'Marry, and settle down.' Months of restless unease, leading to this inevitable moment, had been spent wandering about the hills, mournfully whispering, and watching the high open fields stepping away eastwards under gigantic clouds…

That first day alone – and now I was really alone at last – steadily declined in excitement and vigour. As I tramped through the dust towards the Wiltshire Downs a growing reluctance weighed me down. White elder-blossom and dog-roses hung in the hedges, blank as unwritten paper, and the hot empty road – there were few motor cars then – reflected Sunday's waste and indifference. High sulky summer sucked me towards it, and I offered no resistance at all. Through the solitary morning and afternoon I found myself longing for some opposition or rescue, for the sound of hurrying footsteps coming after me and family voices calling me back.

None came. I was free. I was affronted by freedom. The day's silence said, Go where you will. It's all yours. You asked for it. It's up to you now. You're on your own, and nobody's going to stop you. As I walked, I was taunted by echoes of home, by the tinkling sounds of the kitchen, shafts of sun from the windows falling across the familiar furniture, across the bedroom and the bed I had left.

When I judged it to be tea-time I sat on an old stone wall and opened my tin of treacle biscuits. As I ate them I could hear mother banging the kettle on the hob and my brothers rattling their tea-cups. The biscuits tasted sweetly of the honeyed squalor of home – still only a dozen miles away.

I might have turned back then if it hadn't been for my brothers, but I couldn't have borne the look on their faces. So I got off the wall and went on my way.

Key Reading

Recount texts

This text is a **recount**. Its **purpose** is to retell events in an entertaining way.

The main features of this text are:
- It is told mainly in the **past tense**, for example, 'I *turned* the corner.'
- It generally describes events in **time order**, but includes a flashback.
- It uses **time connectives**, for example, 'Through the solitary morning and afternoon…'
- It uses **descriptive language** to bring the events alive, such as adjectives, powerful verbs and imagery, for example: 'High *sulky* summer *sucked* me towards it.'
- It uses **paragraphs** to mark a change of focus. For example, paragraph 5 marks a change in focus from the past to the journey ahead.

1 Find two examples of the **simple past** tense, and two examples of the **past perfect** tense in this text. Try to explain why the tense has been used in each case.

2 At what time, day, month and year is the start of this recount set? What are we told about the place and the landscape?

3 Find two sentences with a powerful description. Identify the types of words or phrases that make it so effective – for example, adjective, verb, simile.

4 Draw a timeline to represent the bare bones of this extract. How will you represent the flashback on your timeline?

Mark the paragraph breaks with a double line. Write a note explaining why the author has started a new paragraph at each point.

Grammar for reading

The most common tense used to refer to a specific event in the past is the **simple past** tense. For example, 'By the time I *arrived* home, it *was* five o'clock.'

The **past perfect** ('had' + past tense) is used to refer to what happened before events described in the past. For example, 'He *had tidied* up by the time I arrived.'

Purpose

5 Autobiographical writing, like this extract, can have many different purposes.

a) Why do you think Laurie Lee has written this account?

b) Think of three other reasons why people write accounts of their lives.

c) How do these different purposes affect the style of writing that results?

Reading for meaning

6 This life-changing day, and the build-up to it, evokes many different feelings in the author. Chart any changes in his mood, both before this day and through the day, by drawing up a table like the one below:

Time	Mood	Evidence
months before	restless, trapped	'months of restless unease' (lines 30–31)

7 '…it never occurred to me that others had done this before me' (lines 24–25). What does Laurie Lee mean?

8 What is the effect of the short sentences in line 46?

9 All these movement verbs are used in the extract: 'step', 'wander', 'tramp', 'hurry', 'walk', 'went on my way'.

  a) How does each verb describe movement and the author's mood differently?

  b) Add 'stride', 'plod' and 'scuttle' to the list. What would you use these words to describe?

10 Imagine that you were turning Laurie Lee's book into a stage play. Improvise this opening scene in groups of four. Think about:
- how you could suggest what has led up to this event (see paragraph 4)
- how you would present Laurie Lee's actual departure
- how you could suggest his change in mood through the day
- whether you would include any speech
- what props or scenery and lighting you would use.

On the streets

Focus on: Describing a writer's style

How do you describe in detail the style of a piece of writing?

11 First, read the extract carefully. Look out for the following features:

- **vocabulary** – Plain or highly descriptive? Any powerful words used? Any sound effects?
- **imagery** – Any similes, metaphors and personification used?
- **sentence structure/punctuation** – Length of sentences? Complex or simple? Variety?
- **formality** – Is the language informal, formal or a mixture?
- **narrative perspective** – From what point of view is the passage written?
- **structure** – How is the text structured as a whole? (Chronologically, with flashbacks, etc.)

Look again at paragraphs 4, 5 and 6. Make notes on each of these features and comment on their effect.

For example, you could make notes on the start of paragraph 4 like this:

Lee writes from the distant perspective of later years. This allows him to contrast his wisdom now with his youth then

formal language used throughout, for example, 'traditional forces'. This gives the account authority

> I was propelled, of course, by the traditional forces that had sent many generations along this road – by the small tight valley closing in around one…

'propelled' suggests being forced out strongly – a good word to use in this context

personification used very well – both the valley and the cottage are described as if pinning him down

12 Read through these notes on paragraph 4 again.

   a) Which features in the bulleted list above does each relate to?

   b) Which part of the notes above identify the feature? Which parts describe its effect?

Key Writing

To make points clearly when writing an essay, you can use the 'Point Evidence Comment' technique:
- first state your **point** clearly
- next, quote the **evidence** from the text – the key words only, put in inverted commas
- finally, add a **comment** on the effect – saying how well the feature works, or adding a personal comment on its effect.

There are different ways in which you could introduce evidence:
- using a colon, for example:
  Lee sometimes uses short sentences for effect: 'None came. I was free.'
- using an **introductory phrase**, for example, 'like', 'such as'
- integrating the quotation in the sentence, for example:
  The sentences that start the next paragraph, 'None came. I was free', are deliberately short.

Wr17 **13 a)** Two writers have analysed Laurie Lee's use of personification (below). Which analysis is more effective, and why?

A

Laurie Lee uses personification very effectively in this extract. The valley 'stifling the breath with its mossy mouth' and the cottage walls narrowing like 'arms' both paint a picture of a living being deliberately crushing the young man and not allowing him to escape.

B

Lee 'was propelled' to leave home by 'the small tight valley', which was 'stifling the breath with its mossy mouth'. He was also propelled by 'the cottage walls narrowing like the arms of an iron maiden'. These are both good examples of personification.

b) Using your notes, write a short essay (300–350 words) analysing the style of paragraphs 4–6 of the extract. Remember to:
- use 'Point Evidence Comment'
- organise your writing in paragraphs so that they cover the six features of style described on page 116, i.e. one short paragraph per feature
- introduce the evidence in varied ways, and punctuate the quotations correctly.

4 Unit 5 Assignment: Homeless

On the streets

Assessment Focuses

▸ **AF3** Organise and present whole texts effectively, sequencing and structuring information, ideas and events

▸ **AF4** Construct paragraphs and use cohesion within and between paragraphs

You: are designing a website for a homelessness charity.

Your task: to turn some notes from an interview with a homeless person into an effective personal story for the website.

Quotes

"I was too proud to contact my parents."

"That was the worst night of my life. I didn't want to wake up."

"I had all my possessions in a single bag."

"I reckon I'm one of the lucky ones."

"I didn't think I could sink any lower. Begging was so humiliating."

"It was so weird feeling the cool air on my face."

"I've never felt so tired, dirty and hungry."

Key facts

- Name: Terry Davis
- Age: 20
- Present address: Hostel for the homeless, Dudley

Recent history

- June 2004, T. quit job – row with manager. T. couldn't pay rent and bills
- July, left flat, stayed on friends' floors in Dudley, 'overstayed welcome'
- All hostels full – slept in car parks in August
- Befriended by other homeless people
- Had to beg to get food
- Sept. – got some benefit money and a room came up in a hostel

Family history

- Grew up in comfortable home in countryside
- Parents divorced when T. was 7
- Mum remarried but T. fell out with stepfather
- At 17 got job in garden centre, moved into flat with girlfriend Sasha.

Stage 1

In pairs, discuss what purpose you might have in including Trevor's story on the website. Who would be reading this story?

Now think about how the purpose and audience will affect the kind of recount that you will write. In particular:

- What kind of person will Terry be?
- Will the style be plain and informal, or formal and 'literary'?

Stage 2

Read the four pages of notes from the interview with Terry. Think about how you will organise these notes so that they form the basis of 'Terry's Story'.

Now plan your recount. Organise your notes into what will be four paragraphs. Remember that a new paragraph marks a change of focus.

In your plan, give your paragraphs headings. For example:

- Paragraph 1: A comfortable life
- Paragraph 2: Out on their ears
- Paragraph 3: …

Mark on the plan where you could include some of Terry's quotations.

Stage 3

Now write your recount. Remember:

- Put the events in time order. You could include a flashback for effect – for example, by beginning with Terry as he is now.
- Use connectives (especially of time) to make the sequence of events clear to the reader.
- Include specific names, dates and some telling descriptive details to bring the story alive.
- Write in the third person and the past tense.

Challenge

Imagine that Terry is writing his autobiography. He wants to draw the reader in quickly through the power of the written word.

Choose one incident from your recount that would make a good opening to the autobiography. Rewrite this incident in the first person, making your language and style less formal and more engaging for the reader. You are writing as Terry.

Unit 6 Your life

1 Mother and daughter

Aims

- Read a newspaper interview of a mother and daughter
- Explore how discursive texts present people's views
- Present a balanced report on your friends' views (R2, Wr16)

The following text comes from *The Daily Telegraph*.

**Katie believes in God and marriage.
Her mother doesn't.**

KATIE Lodwidge's life revolves around hair, make-up, shoes and clothes, according to her mother.

The 15-year-old reads teenage magazines, talks for hours to her friends, enjoys dance, singing and aerobics and hates tidying her bedroom.

5

But behind this façade of normal teenage behaviour, Katie has developed a keen sense of morality and conservative social attitudes which contrast with the more liberal views of her mother, Alyson Pratt, 38.

10

Katie believes strongly in marriage and hopes to walk down the aisle one day. She feels that it is all right for people to have children outside marriage if they love each other and are in a stable relationship, but she wants to get married first.

This surprises Alyson, a legal secretary, who says she did not marry Katie's father. 'I don't believe in marriage in this day and age because things have changed and so many marriages end in the heartache and nastiness of divorce.'

15

Katie believes in God. Her mother is an atheist. Katie is proud to be British, her mother is stumped by the question. Katie wants Britain to become more integrated with the rest of Europe whereas her mother is firmly against it.

At home in Locksheath, near Fareham, in Hampshire, yesterday mother and daughter discovered new things about each other. Katie says abortion is a serious step only to be undertaken when there is a good reason. Alyson supports abortion on demand because it is a woman's right to choose.

On drugs the teenager is against legalisation of cannabis because it will encourage young people to experiment and fail to stop the dealers who will buy up supplies to sell cut-price on the streets. She wants tougher penalties for drugs. Her mother says cannabis should be legalised. 'People are going to get hold of it, whether it is against the law or not.'

On tougher penalties for crime their views coincide and both would like to see the death penalty brought back for child killers.

Their views diverge again on whether there should be tougher penalties to discourage under-age sex. Katie thinks there should be, to act as a deterrent. Her mother says tougher sanctions would make no difference. 'If they want to have sex they will do it and I blame parents. It's up to parents to educate their children about the dangers of under-age sex, not schools. I know of people who allow their 13- and 14-year old daughters to entertain boyfriends in their bedrooms. That will never happen in this house!'

They agree to differ on the war in Iraq. 'People are still dying and when I read about what America has done in the Middle East, I think they are both as bad as each other,' says Katie. Her mother backs the attack and says continuing casualties are regrettable but inevitable as peace is restored.

'I am surprised by some of my daughter's views. I had no idea she was thinking so deeply about the issues,' says Alyson. Katie wants to get back to washing her hair.

Key Reading

Discursive texts

This is a **discursive** text. Its **purpose** is to present different views as fairly as possible.

The main features of this text are:

- Its **form**, which is a series of points organised into **paragraphs**. For example, the fourth paragraph presents Katie's views on marriage.
- It is written in the **present tense**, for example, 'Katie *believes* in God.'
- It presents **points** supported by **evidence** or **reasons**, for example, 'Alyson supports abortion on demand because it is a woman's right to choose.'
- It uses **formal language**, for example, 'Katie has developed a keen sense of morality.'
- It uses **sentence signposts** to introduce the points of view, for example, 'Katie says abortion is a serious step…'

1 Find evidence for each of the features above in the first half of the text. Write up your notes into five short paragraphs, one on each feature.
- Use a topic sentence to make it clear what each paragraph is about.
- Refer to at least two examples from the text as evidence.
- Give at least one reason why each feature is used.

Purpose

2 This article accompanied a larger article reporting the results of a nationwide survey of young people's social attitudes. Why do you think the newspaper added this article to the main report?

Reading for meaning

3 Why is Katie's 'normal teenager behaviour' described as a 'façade' (line 6)?

4 Many issues are explored in this interview. Discuss with a partner how you could display mother and daughter's views on all these issues.

    a) Consider the following options: bullet points, a table or a spidergram.

    b) Use your agreed method to summarise the main points of the article. Include any reasons that Katie and Alyson give for their views.

5 a) What does the writer mean when she says that Alyson is 'stumped by the question' about being proud to be British (line 19)? What do you think Alyson's answer actually was?

    b) Explain what the phrase 'agree to differ' means, referring to the example in the text (line 43).

6 Why does the writer wait until half way through the article to tell us where Katie and Alyson live (line 22)?

7
> The writer of this article is careful to present the views of Katie and her mother in a balanced way. This fairness is shown both in the amount of coverage given to each person's views, and in the way they are reported.

    a) Find an example from the text to illustrate the above statement.

    b) Imagine that you were writing a report critical of young people's views. How could you change your example so that it was biased rather than fair?

8 Analyse the punctuation in paragraph 10 (lines 35–42). Identify each punctuation mark and explain why it has been used.

9 a) Explain the term 'ring composition' with reference to this article.

b) How effective is the ring composition here? Give your reasons.

> **ring composition** using the same idea to begin and end a text so that they join up to form a 'ring'

Focus on: Presenting views

There are different ways of contrasting people's views in a discursive text. For example:

| Katie believes in God. Her mother is an atheist. | — two short sentences, each beginning with the person's name; the contrast in views is **implied** |

| Katie wants Britain to be more integrated with the rest of Europe, whereas her mother is firmly against it. | — here the connective 'whereas' signals the contrast; the contrast is **explicit** |

10 Discuss these two ways of contrasting Katie's views and those of her mother.

a) Which is the clearer method? Which is more stylish?

b) Which method is preferred by the author of the article? Why do you think this is?

Connectives such as 'whereas' are very useful in making contrasts clear to the reader. Other connectives that can be used in this way include 'but', 'yet', 'while', 'however', 'on the other hand' and 'by contrast'.

11 In pairs, find a subject that you disagree about. Then write one sentence that includes both your views. Rewrite the sentence three more times, using a different way of signalling the contrast each time.

You can add further variety to your discursive text like this:

- Points of view can be **quoted directly** or **reported** (see 'Grammar for reading' below).
- Use **different reporting verbs**, as too much use of 'said' or 'say' makes your writing dull and repetitive. Some other verbs you could use are:

argue	claim	emphasise	counter
point out	reply	believe	state

- **Rephrase the sentence** completely to avoid using a reporting verb, for example: 'According to her mother…', 'Katie has a different point to make:…'.

12 Scan the newspaper article. How many different reporting verbs have been used? What effect does this have?

13 The extract on the right is from a survey article on young people's attitudes to the royal family. Read it and then imagine what Katie and her mum think about the subject. Add a short paragraph to the interview, focusing on presenting their views in a clear but elegant way.

> Two thirds (66 per cent) wanted to keep the Royal Family rather than have a presidential system.

Grammar for reading

Direct speech is when the exact words that the speaker or writer uses are quoted, for example: 'He said, "We should be allowed to do what we want."'

Reported speech is when the words used are only referred to, or reported, for example: 'He said that they should be allowed to do what they wanted.'

Note that in reported speech:
- no inverted commas are needed
- no comma is needed after the reporting clause 'said that…'
- the pronoun and the tense of the verb often need changing.

Exploring further: Direct and reported speech

Sometimes it is effective to use both direct and reported speech when presenting a point. For example: 'Her mother says cannabis should be legalised. "People are going to get hold of it, whether it is against the law or not."' Note that you do not need to repeat 'she says' when introducing the direct speech, as it is clear from the context.

14 Rewrite the last paragraph of the article so that it becomes a mixture of direct and reported speech.

Key Writing

R2, Wr16

15 a) In groups, discuss your own views on these issues:
- marriage
- penalties for crime
- banning smoking in public.

Take notes on everyone's views.

b) Then write up your notes as a discursive text.

Remember to:
- use connectives if you want to signal contrasting views
- use sentence signposts to introduce new views/topics
- include both direct and reported speech – and a mixture of the two for some points
- vary your reporting verbs
- present everyone's views fairly – including your own.

2 Junk the ads?

Aims

- Read some points of view about fast-food advertising
- Make a counter-argument to a view that has been expressed (Wr14)
- Compare different points of view (S&L5)

Health and consumer organisations are calling for a ban on junk-food adverts in an attempt to tackle the rise of health-related problems. Here are five email letters written as part of this debate.

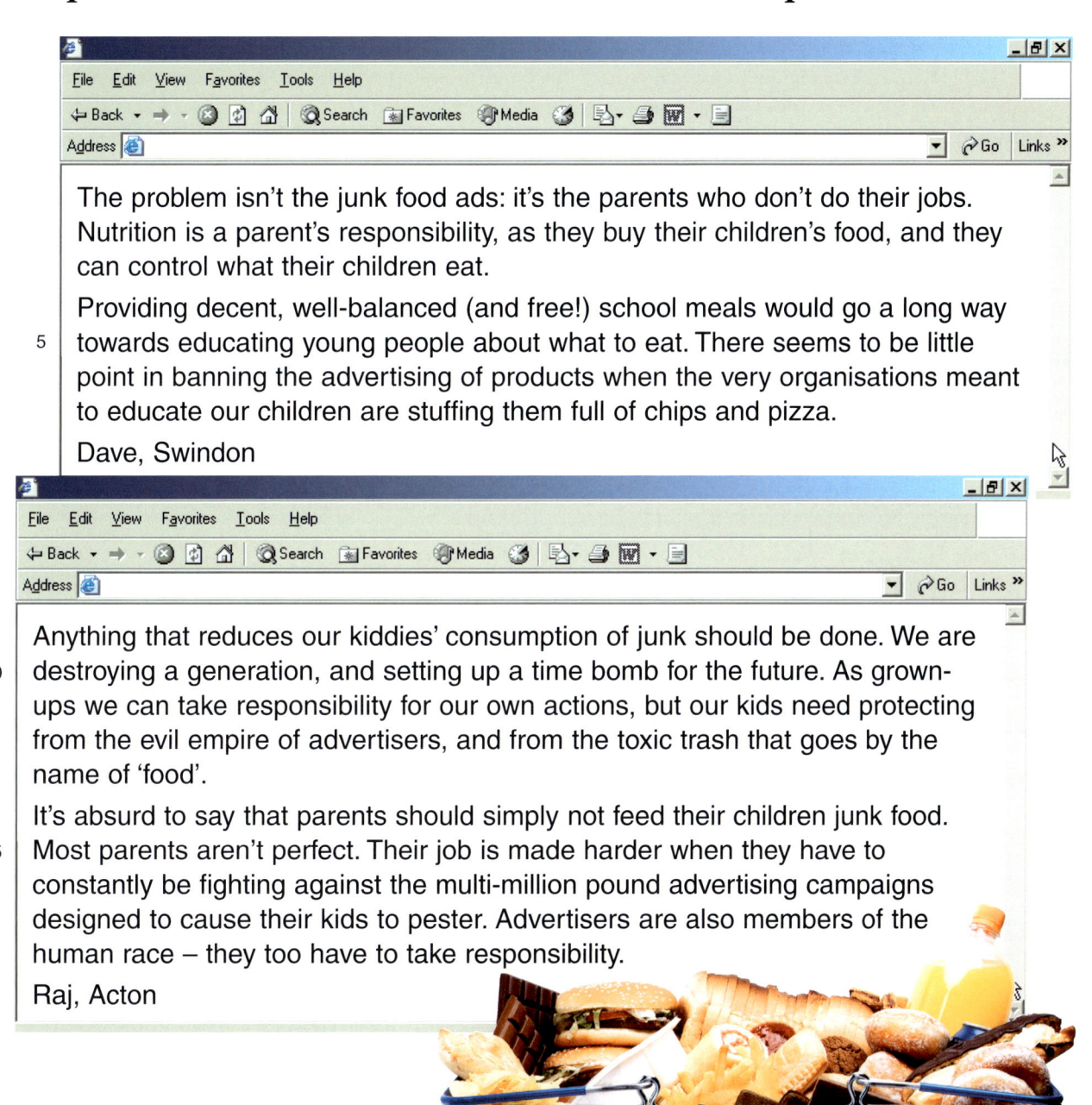

The problem isn't the junk food ads: it's the parents who don't do their jobs. Nutrition is a parent's responsibility, as they buy their children's food, and they can control what their children eat.

5 Providing decent, well-balanced (and free!) school meals would go a long way towards educating young people about what to eat. There seems to be little point in banning the advertising of products when the very organisations meant to educate our children are stuffing them full of chips and pizza.

Dave, Swindon

10 Anything that reduces our kiddies' consumption of junk should be done. We are destroying a generation, and setting up a time bomb for the future. As grown-ups we can take responsibility for our own actions, but our kids need protecting from the evil empire of advertisers, and from the toxic trash that goes by the name of 'food'.

It's absurd to say that parents should simply not feed their children junk food.
15 Most parents aren't perfect. Their job is made harder when they have to constantly be fighting against the multi-million pound advertising campaigns designed to cause their kids to pester. Advertisers are also members of the human race – they too have to take responsibility.

Raj, Acton

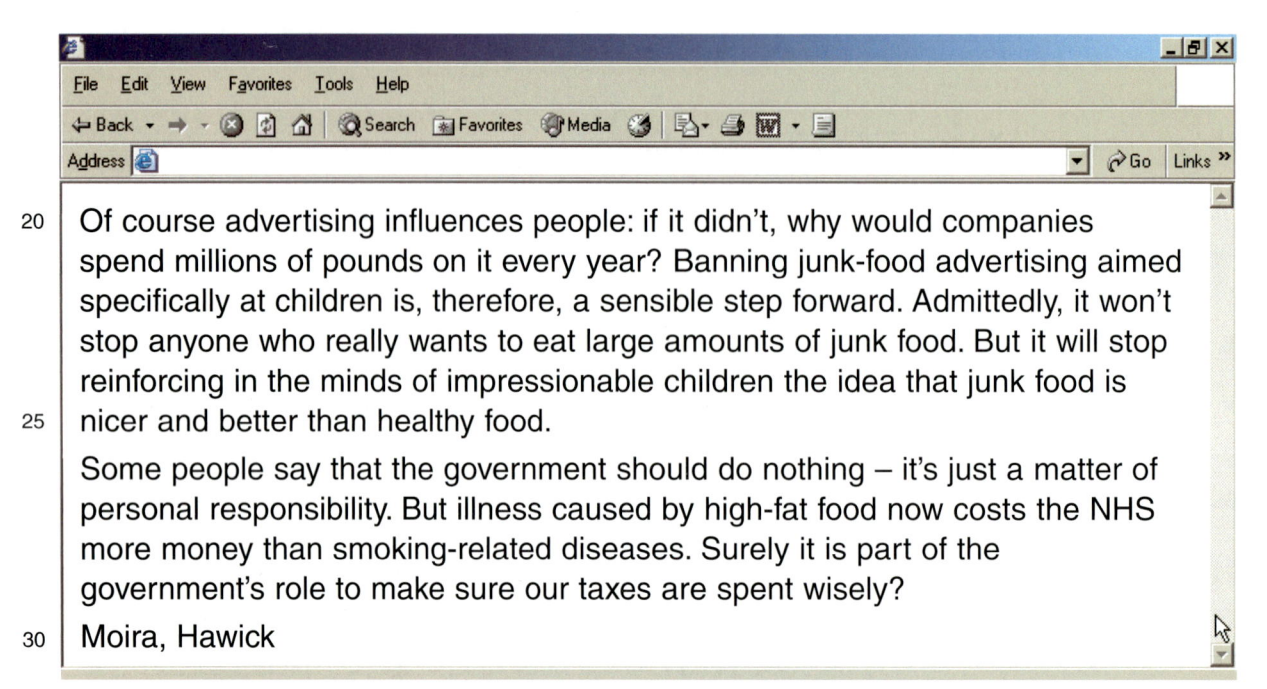

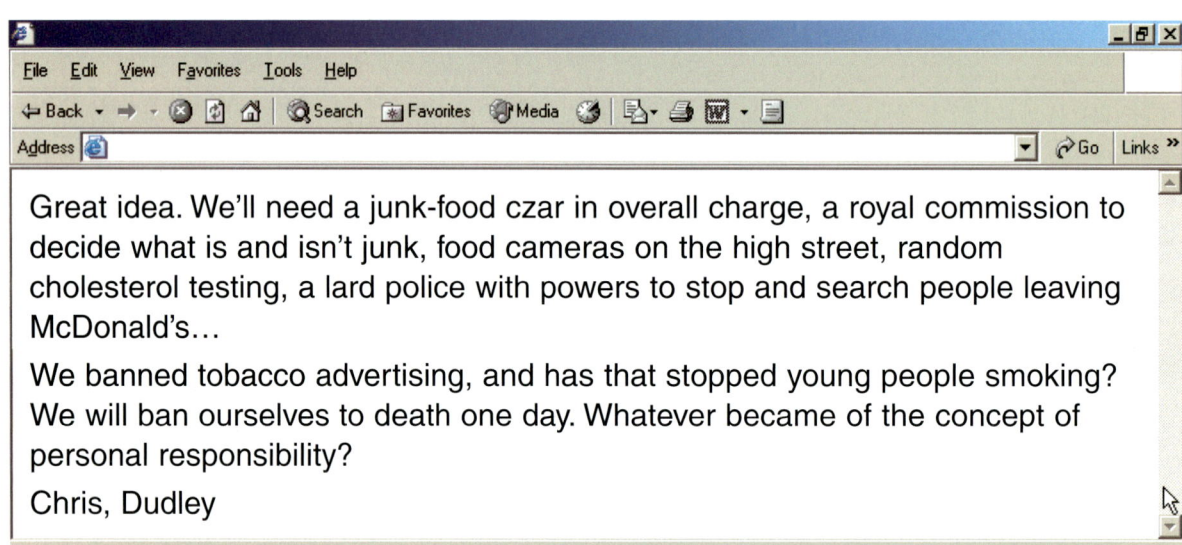

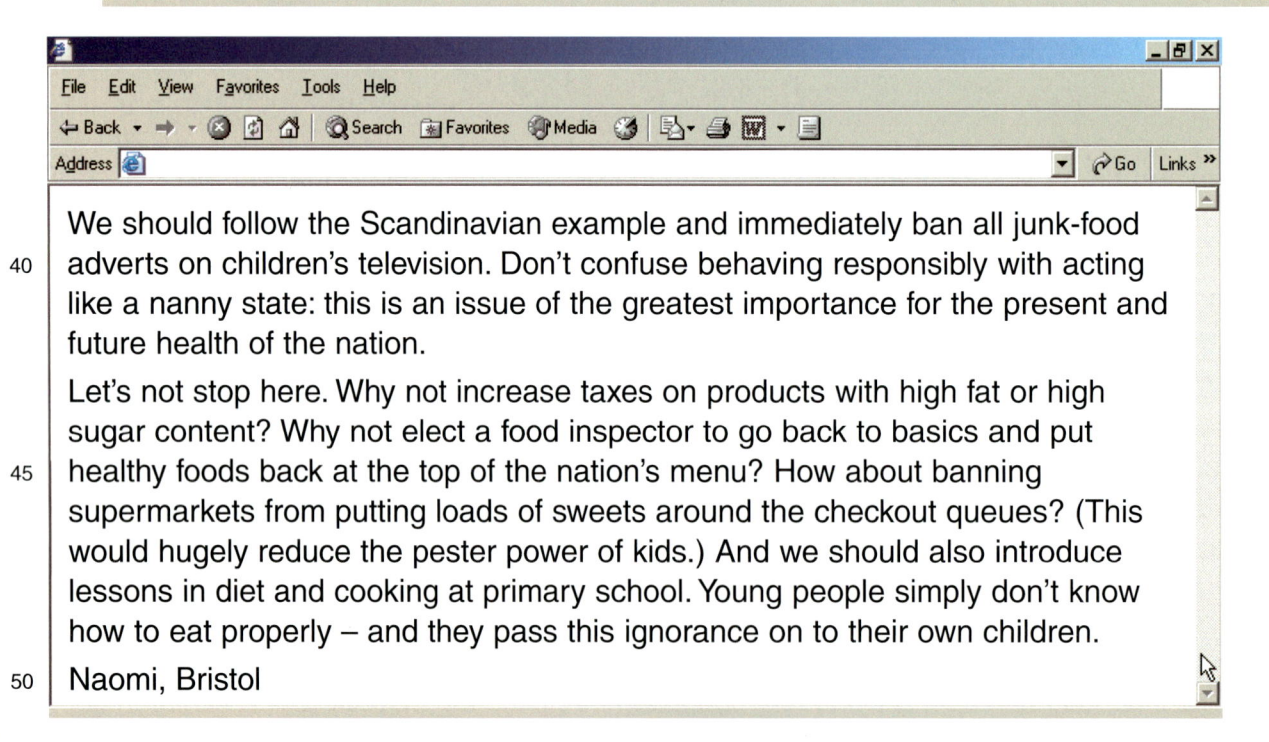

20　Of course advertising influences people: if it didn't, why would companies spend millions of pounds on it every year? Banning junk-food advertising aimed specifically at children is, therefore, a sensible step forward. Admittedly, it won't stop anyone who really wants to eat large amounts of junk food. But it will stop reinforcing in the minds of impressionable children the idea that junk food is
25　nicer and better than healthy food.

　　Some people say that the government should do nothing – it's just a matter of personal responsibility. But illness caused by high-fat food now costs the NHS more money than smoking-related diseases. Surely it is part of the government's role to make sure our taxes are spent wisely?

30　Moira, Hawick

　　Great idea. We'll need a junk-food czar in overall charge, a royal commission to decide what is and isn't junk, food cameras on the high street, random cholesterol testing, a lard police with powers to stop and search people leaving McDonald's…

35　We banned tobacco advertising, and has that stopped young people smoking? We will ban ourselves to death one day. Whatever became of the concept of personal responsibility?

　　Chris, Dudley

　　We should follow the Scandinavian example and immediately ban all junk-food
40　adverts on children's television. Don't confuse behaving responsibly with acting like a nanny state: this is an issue of the greatest importance for the present and future health of the nation.

　　Let's not stop here. Why not increase taxes on products with high fat or high sugar content? Why not elect a food inspector to go back to basics and put
45　healthy foods back at the top of the nation's menu? How about banning supermarkets from putting loads of sweets around the checkout queues? (This would hugely reduce the pester power of kids.) And we should also introduce lessons in diet and cooking at primary school. Young people simply don't know how to eat properly – and they pass this ignorance on to their own children.

50　Naomi, Bristol

Key Reading

Argument texts

These are **argument** texts. Their **purpose** is to argue for a particular point of view.

The main features of these texts are:

- Their **form**, which is a series of points backed up by reasons or **evidence**. For example, Dave's first point is that parents are the problem.
- They use **topic sentences** to introduce each main point, for example, 'Some people say that the government should do nothing…'
- They contain a mixture of **formal** and **informal** language. For example, 'The problem isn't the junk food ads' is written in informal language.
- They use either a **reasonable** or a **highly emotive tone**. For example, 'the evil empire of advertisers' is an emotive phrase.
- They use **logical connectives** to signpost the argument for the reader, for example, '*but* illness caused by high-fat food now costs the NHS…'

1 Find evidence for each of the features above in the first three emails. Write up your notes into five short paragraphs, one on each feature.
- Use a topic sentence to make it clear what each paragraph is about.
- Refer to at least two examples as evidence.
- Give a reason why each feature is used.

Purpose

2 Sum up the main purpose of all these emails in a single sentence. (There are two distinct views you should identify in your sentence.)

Reading for meaning

3 Some of Raj's language is highly emotive.

a) Identify which words and phrases are chosen especially to sway the audience's emotions.

b) Make a comment on the effect of each one.

4 Moira makes her argument as reasonable as possible. Comment on how the language in each of these sentences represents this reasonable tone:

a) 'Banning junk-food advertising aimed specifically at children is, therefore, a sensible step forward.' (lines 21–22)

b) 'Admittedly, it won't stop anyone who really wants to eat large amounts of junk food.' (lines 22–23)

c) 'Surely it is part of the government's role to make sure our taxes are spent wisely?' (lines 28–29)

5 Identify one other email written in an emotive tone, and one other email written using a reasonable tone. Overall, which approach do you think is more effective in putting an argument across? Give your reasons.

6 Which writers use the first person plural ('we' and 'our') in their emails? Explain the purpose of this and whether it is effective in each case.

7 '**Irony** is a very effective technique when you want to counter an opponent's views.'
Explain this statement by referring to Chris's use of irony in her email.

> **irony** a type of humour in which words are used to mean the opposite of what they appear to mean

8 Draw up a table with the following headings to compare the five emails:
- For or against a ban on junk food?
- Emotive or reasonable tone?
- Any reasons or evidence given?
- Formal or informal language?
- How clear and logical?
- Any other proposals made?
- How effective an argument overall?

Try to give an example or a reason to back up your judgement in each case.

9 What is your own view on banning advertising of junk food?
Has your view been altered by the arguments in any of these emails?
Write a paragraph to summarise your view.

Focus on: Counter-arguments

'Attack is the best form of defence.' This can apply to argument texts. Sometimes a good way of making your points is to attack, or **counter**, your opponents' argument. You can do this in different ways:

You can simply **state the opponent's view and deny it**, or give a reason why it is wrong – for example, 'Some people say… but the fact is that…'

Or you can use stronger tactics and **make your opponent's argument seem ridiculous** by:

1 **Saying that they – or their argument – are illogical**.
   The idea is to make your argument the only reasonable one. For example: 'They are blind to logic and common sense', 'Any sane person would…'.

2 **Ridiculing the opposition**.
   Emotive or biased language is used to put the opposition in a bad light. For example: 'This lunatic fringe', 'Can you really trust people who…?'.

3 **Exaggerating the opposition's case**.
   Putting the opponents' points in an exaggerated way undermines them by making them sound silly or extreme.

10 a) Find two examples in the emails where the opponent's view is simply countered. Then find two ways in which the opponent's view is made to seem ridiculous.

   b) Which of these is the more effective technique, in your opinion?

Wr14 **11** Here are some arguments against a ban on fox hunting. Your task is to write an email presenting a counter-argument – for a ban.

- Fox hunting is a traditional country pursuit supported by 60% of people in hunting areas – city-dwellers should not interfere.
- Fishing is just as cruel as fox hunting – why isn't that criticised?
- A foxhound kills a fox quickly and cleanly; shooting can cause foxes slow and painful deaths.

a) Brainstorm some arguments against fox hunting. Then pick the three best arguments and write a short paragraph on each. Remember to use *either* a reasonable tone or an emotive tone – keep it consistent.

b) Make sure you counter at least two of the opponents' arguments in at least one of your paragraphs. Are you going to counter the point directly, or make the opponents seem ridiculous for holding this view?

You may like to use these phrases:

Good phrases to counter an argument:

The argument that... simply doesn't work.

It isn't the case that...

The main point is not..., but...

Good phrases to make the opponent seem ridiculous:

These absurd people say that...

People must be crazy if they think that...

What sane person would...?

Key Speaking and Listening

12 a) Four students are going to read out their arguments against fox hunting. Your job is to listen to them carefully and compare them. Jot down some notes as you listen.

b) Then organise your notes in a table, like the one below:

	Student 1	Student 2	Student 3	Student 4
What main arguments are used?				
How do they counter the opposing argument?				
Are any powerful words or phrases used?				
Is the tone reasonable or rhetorical?				
Is the argument well organised?				
Comment on the overall effectiveness of the argument				

c) Be ready to share your views and to use a reasonable tone to express your argument.

Exploring further: Logical feedback

13 As you prepare to use your table to give feedback on each student's argument, think about how you can include logical connectives to signpost your views and make them clear.

Try to use some of the following connectives:
- But…
- However…
- So…
- Therefore…
- Furthermore…

3 How to party

Aims

- Read an article about coping with parties
- Understand the impact that complex sentences can make on your writing (S1)
- Write a piece of humorous advice in an impersonal style (Wr15)

This text comes from a supplement in *The Guardian*.

How to...go to a party

Parties peak between the ages of two and seven, where the high point is cake. There is another peak between 17 and 22, where the high point is the snog. The final peak is between 60 and 75, when cake makes a comeback. After that, the men start dying and the fun goes out of it.

5 There is no greater challenge in modern life than entering a party where you know nobody and everyone is locked into hugely enjoyable conversations with people they love enormously. You have three options at this point. The first and best one is to go home immediately and watch television. However, you will then be tortured by the thought
10 that this was actually the party of a lifetime, where you were on the cusp of meeting the person of your dreams and drinking champagne with them until dawn (someone else can drink the plastic bottle of cider you brought with you).

The next option is to step confidently into the room and say 'Excuse
15 me' as you push past various groups as if you were just feet away from joining the group that's waiting so expectantly for you. Keep saying 'Excuse me' until you reach a wall and then turn around and make your way back. Do this until you meet someone else doing it or it's time to go home.

20 Option three is to hack your way across the room to the table on which the nibbles are placed. You then have to pretend to be enormously hungry and start eating chopped carrots. If there is nobody at the party you know, you will then eat more carrots than you have eaten up to that point in your adult life. If it's a bowl of cheesy Wotsits, remember
25 that you're likely to be covered head to foot in orange powder by the time you finish.

The nibbles table is the service station for party conversations, so it's often a good place to start conversations with people who are desperate to escape the conversation they've just come from. One good opening
30 line is, "Do you know, from the other side of the room, I thought these carrots were cheesy Wotsits." This also serves as a good closing line.

There are only three cool ways of leaving a party: you can leave it propped up by your mates; you can leave it with someone gorgeous on your arm; or you can pretend you're going on to a cool club. Remember,
35 it's very difficult to pretend that you're going on somewhere exciting if you're sober, by yourself and covered in Wotsits dust.

This leaflet was handed out to young children at school.

Be Safe At Your Firework Party

We all want to enjoy our firework parties this November.

But kids! You must follow a few simple safety rules.

Remember, Remember:

* Light sparklers one at a time. Three sparklers together give off the same heat as a blow-torch. That's hot!!
* Always wear gloves and be very sensible.
* Don't wave your sparkler around where there are other people.
* Never approach a firework or throw an old firework onto the fire.
* Only an adult should light a firework.
* Stand well back.

BE SAFE. BE SURE. BE HAPPY.

Key Reading

Advice texts

These texts are **advice** texts. Their **purpose** is to give you advice and persuade you to take it.

The main features of *How to… go to a party* are:

- Its **form**, which is a series of **points in a logical order**. For example, the first point made is about the ages when parties are important.
- It uses **direct address** to the reader, for example, '*You* have three options at this point…'
- It uses **causal connectives** to show the consequences of actions, for example, '*If it's a bowl of cheesy Wotsits*, remember…'
- It adopts an **impersonal tone** to suggest authority, for example, 'There are only three cool ways of leaving a party…'
- It uses **humour**, for example, 'After that, the men start dying and the fun goes out of it.'

1 Identify another example in *How to… go to a party* of each of the features of advice texts listed above.

2 Draw up a 'main features' panel in a similar way for the *Be Safe At Your Firework Party* leaflet. (You may decide to change some of the features.) Give an example of each feature and comment on its effect.

Purpose

3 a) What is the main purpose of *How to… go to a party*?

b) What is the main purpose of *Be Safe At Your Firework Party*?

Reading for meaning

4 Draw a text skeleton to summarise the content of *How to… go to a party*. The main points go on the left, and the supporting points or further detail on the right.

a) The skeleton for the article has been started for you below. Write it out and complete it to create a full set of notes on the article.

1. The ages when parties are important
   - age 2-7, high point = cake
   - age 17-22, high point = snog
   - age 60-75, high point = cake
   - after that, no fun

b) Write out the topic sentence of each paragraph. How do these relate to the main points of the article in your skeleton plan?

5 One technique the writer uses is to give each paragraph a powerful ending, or 'punchline'. Choose four paragraphs and explain why the writer has ended them the way he has.

6 'The author uses imagery in a colourful way in this article.'
Explain this statement with reference to the metaphor 'hack your way across the room' (line 20) and the reference to the nibbles table as the 'service station' for party conversations.

7 Cheesy Wotsits becomes a **motif** in this article.

a) Why do you think the author keeps returning to them? Is this effective?

> **motif** a theme or idea that is revisited or elaborated on in a piece of writing or music

b) How could you use the ideas in this article as the basis for a TV advert for Cheesy Wotsits? The punchline could be:

'Cheesy Wotsits – they're what parties are for.'

8 In pairs, discuss what makes *How to… go to a party* funny. Agree on two main sources of humour.

9 Draw up a table to compare these features of the two advice texts:
- subject matter
- audience
- purpose
- design/format
- sentence structure
- overall structure
- humour
- style (language, use of direct address, tone, imperatives).

Focus on: Using complex sentences

Good writers use **complex** sentences, as they make the link between ideas in a sentence clear. For example:

'The nibbles table is the service station for party conversations, *so* it's often a good place to start conversations'

Note the connective 'so', which introduces the subordinate clause. It shows the link with the main clause.

10 a) Which other connectives could you use in the sentence above without altering the overall meaning?

b) Write two complex sentences beginning 'The Wotsits'. Choose two different connectives from this panel to link your sentences. Now try moving the clauses around to vary the rhythm or emphasis and comment on the result.

> when
> before
> because
> although
> as if
> as soon as

Sometimes subordinate clauses can be **embedded** in the main clause:
'The nibbles table, *which was tucked behind the door*, was almost empty. But Maria, *feeling tired*, left early.'

11 Redraft the two sentences below so that they each have an embedded clause. Which version do you prefer in each case?
- The bus driver took a taxi home because he was exhausted.
- Having forgotten his glasses, Greg couldn't read the notice on the door.

12 Think up four complex sentences based on the two simple sentences below. Try varying the order of the main and subordinate clauses or adding details. Be prepared to explain why your sentences are better than the original.

> Mike and Anna turned up at the party.
> Anna decided to leave.

Exploring further: Punctuating complex sentences

When a complex sentence *begins* with the subordinate clause, a comma is used to end that clause. The comma marks the boundary between the subordinate clause and the main clause:

> 'If it's a bowl of cheesy Wotsits, remember that you're likely to be covered…'

When a complex sentence *ends* with the subordinate clause, a comma separates the clauses only if a break is needed.

13 Which of these sentences need a comma between the clauses?
- You shouldn't run before you can walk.
- He failed to get a medal although he was only just in fourth place.
- If you go ahead with this you might regret it.

Key Writing

14 Write a humorous piece in the style of the article on pages 136–137 called 'How to… dance'. It should be four or five paragraphs long.

a) Discuss with a partner some advice points that you could give about dancing. (You will need to decide whether you are advising adults or young people.) Jot these down.

b) Draw up a text skeleton like the one you did to analyse the structure of *How to… go to a party* in question 4. Write the four or five best main points on the left, and list some supporting points or details on the right.

c) As you draft your article, think about the following:
- Is your tone impersonal, to suggest an air of authority? Or is it more informal?
- Have you begun each paragraph with a clear topic sentence?
- Does each paragraph end with a punchline?
- Can you use complex sentences to make the connection between your ideas clear?
- Can you use striking or humorous imagery as a motif in your article?

You may like to begin like this:

> The people who look the most ridiculous on the dance floor…

Your life

4 Unit 6 Assignment: The future is bright

Assessment Focus

▸ AF3 Organise and present whole texts effectively, sequencing and structuring information, ideas and events

> **You:** are writing a letter to a newspaper. The newspaper ran an article arguing that technology will make our lives miserable within twenty years.
>
> **Your task:** to argue that technology will actually make our lives better.

Stage 1

Think of all the ways in which technology may make our lives better over the next twenty years. Draw up a spidergram to list your key points. You could group them in categories, for example:

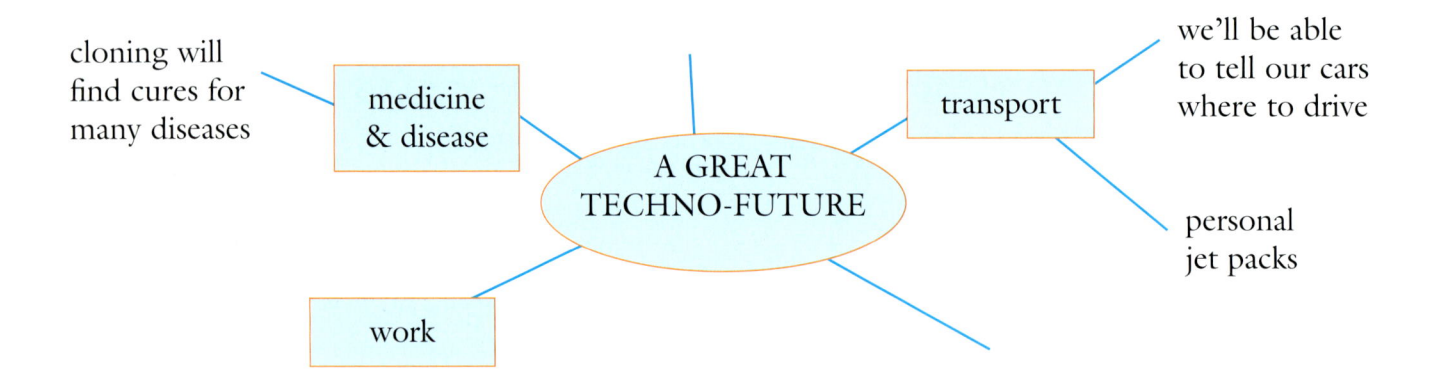

- cloning will find cures for many diseases → medicine & disease
- transport → we'll be able to tell our cars where to drive
- personal jet packs
- work

A GREAT TECHNO-FUTURE

Stage 2

Now plan your letter. Choose the five best points from your spidergram that argue for the benefits of technology in the future. Write down a brief summary of each one.

You are going to write a short paragraph on each main point.

- Begin with a general statement explaining why you are writing, and end with a short conclusion summarising your case.
- Then decide which order you want the paragraphs to go in.
- Next jot down one or two reasons or pieces of evidence or further detail to back up each main point.
- Use a text skeleton to plan your argument.

Stage 3

Now draft your paragraphs. Remember to:

- lay them out like a letter to a newspaper (i.e. begin 'Sir or Madam')
- use topic sentences and signposting to make the direction of the argument clear to the reader
- use formal language
- adopt a reasonable tone
- refer to two or three arguments used in the original article (you will have to imagine what arguments the writer used). Counter these arguments in an effective way.

Challenge

Redraft the first half of your letter so that it has a more emotive tone.

- Select more emotive words and use rhetorical language.
- Rather than countering the opposing argument directly, make it seem ridiculous by using exaggeration or ridicule.

Unit 7 Correspondent

① Letter to Daniel

Aims

- Read a text by a reporter about his son, and past events in his life
- Explore how a writer uses descriptive detail to make key points (Wr11)
- Consider how a writer's point of view affects what he has to say (R11)

In this text, BBC foreign correspondent Fergal Keane writes an imaginary letter for his newborn son.

We have called you Daniel Patrick but I've been told by my Chinese friends that you should have a Chinese name as well and this glorious dawn sky makes me think we'll call you Son of the Eastern Star. So that later, when you and I are far from Asia, perhaps standing on a beach some evening, I can point at the sky and tell you of the Orient and the times and the people we knew there in the last years of the twentieth century.

Your coming has turned me upside down and inside out. So much that seemed essential to me has, in the past few days, taken on a different colour. Like many foreign correspondents I know, I have lived a life that, on occasion, has veered close to the edge: war zones, natural disasters, darkness in all its shapes and forms.

In a world of insecurity and ambition and ego, it's easy to be drawn in, to take chances with our lives, to believe that what we do and what people say about us is reason enough to gamble with death. Now, looking at your sleeping face, inches away from me, listening to your occasional sigh and gurgle, I wonder how I could have ever thought glory and prizes and praise were sweeter than life.

And it's also true that I am pained, perhaps haunted is a better word, by the memory, suddenly so vivid now, of each suffering child I have come across on my journeys. To tell you the truth, it's nearly too much to bear at this moment to even think of children being hurt and abused and killed. And yet looking at you, the images come flooding back. Ten-year-old Andi Mikail dying from napalm burns on a hillside in Eritrea, how his voice cried out, growing ever more faint when the wind blew dust on to his wounds. The two brothers, Domingo and Juste, in Menongue, southern Angola. Juste, two years old and blind, dying from malnutrition, being carried on seven-year-old Domingo's back. And Domingo's words to me, 'He was nice before, but now he has the hunger'.

Last October, in Afghanistan, when you were growing inside your mother, I met Sharja, aged twelve. Motherless, fatherless, guiding me through the grey ruins of her home, everything was gone, she told me. And I knew that, for all her tender years, she had learned more about loss than I would likely understand in a lifetime.

There is one last memory. Of Rwanda, and the churchyard of the parish of Nyarabuye where, in a ransacked classroom, I found a mother and her three young children huddled together where they'd been beaten to death. The children had died holding on to their mother, that instinct we all learn from birth and in one way or another cling to until we die.

Daniel, these memories explain some of the fierce protectiveness I feel for you, the tenderness and the occasional moments of blind terror when I imagine anything happening to you. But there is something more, a story from long ago that I will tell you face to face, father to son, when you are older. It's a very personal story but it's part of the picture. It has to do with the long lines of blood and family, about our lives and how we can get lost in them and, if we're lucky, find our way out again into the sunlight.

It begins thirty-five years ago in a big city on a January morning with snow on the ground and a woman walking to hospital to have her first baby. She is in her early twenties and the city is still strange to her, bigger and noisier than the easy streets and gentle hills of her distant home. She's walking because there is no money and everything of value has been pawned to pay for the alcohol to which her husband has become addicted.

On the way, a taxi driver notices her sitting, exhausted and cold, in the doorway of a shop and he takes her to hospital for free. Later that day, she gives birth to a baby boy and, just as you are to me, he is the best thing she has ever seen. Her husband comes that night and weeps with joy when he sees his son. He is truly happy. Hungover, broke, but in his own way happy, for they were both young and in love with each other and their son.

Key Reading

Recount texts

This text is mainly in the form of a **recount**. Its **purpose** is to tell us about events that have happened.

The main features of this text are:

- It uses **paragraphs** to mark a **change of focus**. For example: The first paragraph deals with the naming of the baby
- It gives specific **dates**, **times** and **names** of people and places, and uses **time connectives**, for example, 'Last *October*, in *Afghanistan*, when you were growing inside your mother, I met *Sharja*, aged *twelve*…'
- It uses **descriptive language** to bring past events to life and convey strong emotion, such as adjectives, adverbs, powerful verbs and sometimes imagery, for example, '…guiding me through the *grey ruins* of her home…'

1. How does the use of pronouns and verb tenses in paragraph 1 make it seem as if Fergal Keane is speaking to his son?

2. The writer deals with four time periods: the first is the future, when he will talk to his grown up child; the next is the present, as he watches his new-born son sleeping. What other times does he refer to?

3. Given what follows, how does the mood of paragraph 1 contrast with what we read later? Identify the particular words and phrases that help to create these contrasting moods.

BBC foreign correspondent Fergal Keane

Purpose

The purpose of this text is to tell us about present – and past – events in a way that makes us think about some important issues.

4 In a small group, discuss the following questions:
   a) Why do you think the writer tells us about the children he has met as a reporter? How does this relate to the audience for his 'letter'?
   b) As a foreign correspondent it is Fergal Keane's job to report from different areas of the world. What four other countries does he refer to in the text? Whereabouts in the world are they situated?

Reading for meaning

5 Fergal Keane was a well established reporter when he wrote this. But he says:

> …looking at your sleeping face, inches away from me, listening to your occasional sigh and gurgle, I wonder how I could have ever thought glory and prizes and praise were sweeter than life…

How has his view about things changed?

6 The text is full of **contrasts** and **comparisons**.
   a) What comparison does he make between the mother and children he sees in Rwanda and himself?
   b) How does he contrast the experiences of the girl, Sharja, he met in Afghanistan?

In each case, find the words that show these things.

7 One of the main themes that runs through this recount is the importance of family. It ends with the tale of another family. Note down who they might be – and why you think this.

8 There are further contrasts in the last two paragraphs. Some relate to place or setting; some relate to people's feelings and behaviour. Can you identify them?

Focus on: Descriptive detail to make a point

Fergal Keane does not want to remember the terrible things he has seen as a reporter, but seeing his own son, he can't help it. So that we can understand how he feels, he tells us about:

> …ten-year-old Andi Mikail dying from napalm burns on a hillside in Eritrea, how his voice cried out, growing ever more faint when the wind blew dust on to his wounds.

9 What two senses does he use in this description to convey the horror of his experience?

10 At other times, for example, at the start of the text, he refers to the senses to create a more pleasant description.

   a) What is the main sense he uses when describing the morning sky?

   b) What senses does he refer to when describing his son, asleep?

The strength of adjectives chosen when detailing experiences is vital to an effective description. For example, Keane describes the ten-year-old's voice 'growing ever more faint'.

11 a) What other adjectives for the level or type of sound/voice could be used?

   Note down as many as you can (for example, 'loud').

   b) How are these different from adjectives such as 'desperate', 'frightened', 'confused', 'relieved', 'joyous' or 'calm'?

   c) Why do you think the adjectives evoking the senses are especially important for a radio report?

12 Write a paragraph or two in which you describe villagers who are trapped on their roofs during a flood.

Try to use adjectives that:

- make use of the concrete, specific things (the sounds the people make; their appearance, etc.)
- focus on more general feelings or ideas (the impression the people give).

For example:

> I could hear their hoarse cries (specific things) as the helicopter approached. Clearly they were desperate (general feelings).

Key Speaking and Listening

Wr11

13 Imagine you are a BBC radio reporter with your own family at home. You are away covering a war in another country and you find a child on his own. Fortunately, he is unhurt, but his family have been captured.

a) Write the two-paragraph opening of a report for the six o'clock news on the radio. Remember to:

- describe the boy
- describe when and where you found him (use time connectives)
- use at least two key senses to add detail and bring it to life
- use different types of adjectives – those that describe people's feelings or the overall impression (for example, 'desperate', 'savage', 'tragic') and those that relate to specific senses (for example, 'loud', 'jagged', 'bloody', 'rough').

b) Add two further paragraphs. Include a contrast between the boy's situation now and what it was like before. (This will mean switching between verb tenses as Fergal Keane does.) For example:
'An hour earlier, the boy had been playing happily with...'

c) Once you have completed your news report, read it out to the rest of the class or a smaller group. Try to 'perform' it as if you are there, rather than just reading it from the page.

Exploring further: Injecting more contrast

14 Think of other contrasts you could add to your report. For example, add two or three sentences on the setting for this news story:

'Once, this battleground was a happy, thriving shopping street. Now, it is...'

15 Listen to a radio reporter delivering a report from a real war zone, and then try to watch the television news on the same night to make comparisons between the two. Which contains more speech? What are the main differences and similarities between the two?

2 Runaway

Aims

- Read an extract from the opening of a novel about South Africa
- Review and develop reading skills related to finding information (R1)
- Use this information when responding to the text
- Write about a text in a considered way

In this extract from her novel *No Turning Back*, South African writer Beverley Naidoo tells a story based on the real-life tales of young children living on the streets.

Tiptoeing towards his mother's bed, Sipho touched the table to steady himself. He held his breath and glanced at the sleeping figures. Two grey shapes which could stir at any time. A small square of plastic above the bed let in the dim early morning light. His mother lay near the edge, one hand resting over her rounded stomach. His stepfather was snoring heavily, a giant of a man stretched across the bed. Each snore shook the stillness of the tiny room. But it was a sigh from his mother that almost made him drop her bag and leave empty-handed. Then his fingers touched the coins. Grasping them, he turned and silently fled. Past the chipped wooden table, the paraffin stove and the pot of cold porridge from the night before. Past his mattress on the floor with the crumpled blanket. Past the orange-crate cupboard and out of the door. He eased it shut, praying that the snoring would cover the sound of creaking hinges.

And then he ran. Keeping his head down, he weaved his way through the patchwork of shacks in the smoky half-light, hoping against hope that no one would call his name. Thin chinks of yellow light and the smell of paraffin lamps behind the sheets of iron and wooden planks showed that people were beginning to rise. Ma and 'him' would have been getting up by now if they had work to go to. Sipho's heart was thumping against his chest. It had been screwed up for the last few days, like the rest of his insides, as tight as a fist. But now it was going wild like the tail of a puppy just let out of a cage. He would have to get it under control before he got to the taxi rank.

Coming out from the shacks, he sprinted past the shop boarded up overnight. He could be seen more easily here. The quickest way would be to cut across by the men's hostel. But that was dangerous. Bullets whistling between the great grim building and the houses nearby had brought death to many people. No one knew when the fighting would start again and Ma had forbidden him to go near the place.

'That bullet won't stop to ask who you are,' Ma had said. But why should he listen to what Ma said any more? Still, it was safer to go the long way round, past his school.

Squares of misty light from houses on each side lit the way and, high above him, electric strips shone dully through the smoke. There were other people on the road already, most walking in the same direction. Sipho slowed down to a half-jog, half-walk. He might draw too much attention to himself if he ran. Passing the crisscross wire fencing around the school, he shifted to the other side of the road. Even though the gate was locked, he could imagine the head teacher suddenly appearing from the low red-brick building and wanting to know where he was going.

The taxi rank was already humming with the early morning crowd milling alongside a line of minibuses. Pavement sellers had already set up their stalls. Some people in the queues carried bags and boxes, perhaps of things to sell in town themselves. With so many taxis, he had to make sure he got in the right one. Glancing briefly at a row of faces he noticed a woman looking at him. She had a baby on her back and seemed about Ma's age. No, he wouldn't ask her. Instead he moved away and asked a young man which was the right queue for Hillbrow.

'Take any one for Jo'burg city centre. It's that side.' The man pointed to where the crowd was thicker.

Slipping behind a line of people, Sipho was pleased he had managed to ask the question so smoothly. If only everyone would move along quickly so he could get inside the taxi. He kept his eyes trained in the direction of the school. What if Ma had woken up? She wouldn't feel up to coming after him, but she would wake his stepfather. If Ma sent him out looking for Sipho, he would be raging mad – even without a drink. Sipho could just imagine him storming through the crowd, shouting his name, demanding if anyone had seen a small boy aged twelve... a boy with big ears, the kind you can get hold of.

Sipho shivered, pulled his woollen cap down lower and clasped his arms around him. It was cold. He should have put on two jumpers.

Correspondent

Key Reading

> ### Narrative texts
>
> This text is a **narrative.** Its **purpose** is to tell a story in an interesting and entertaining way.
>
> The main features of this text are:
>
> - It has a **structure** that includes an **introduction** (the development, complication, climax and resolution of the plot all come later). This opening introduces the main situation and events.
> - It features clearly drawn **characters** in Sipho, his Ma and stepfather, and a **narrator**, who tells the story in either the first person (I/we) or the third person (he/she/it/they), for example, '*Sipho touched* the table to steady himself. *He held* his breath…'
> - **Characters' feelings** are shown or **implied** rather than told directly through the narrative, for example, '…he turned and silently fled' might suggest Sipho is feeling guilty.
> - It uses **expressive and descriptive** language (powerful verbs, nouns, adjectives and figurative language), for example, '…he weaved his way through the patchwork of shacks in the smoky half-light…'

1 Write about the way the opening paragraph sets the scene for us. Include details of the information we are given about the people, the setting and the storyline.

2 Apart from Sipho, Ma and the stepfather, two other characters are briefly mentioned.

   a) One of them is a woman queuing for a taxi. Why is she mentioned, and what is implied by Sipho's reaction to her?

   b) Who is the other character?

3 What can we tell about Sipho's feelings for his mother from this sentence?

'But it was a sigh from his mother that almost made him drop her bag and leave empty-handed.' (lines 7–8)

Purpose

Of course, Beverley Naidoo's *main* purpose is to tell a good story. During the opening she does this by raising questions in the reader's mind. The main question is: 'Why is Sipho running away from home?'

4 In pairs, look through the text again and discuss what you think the answer to this is. Find evidence in the extract to support your views. Be careful – you may find evidence, but it might have more than one meaning.

5 Are there any other questions raised by the start of the novel? What do you predict will happen next?

Reading for meaning

infer – work out or deduce a meaning

In this opening we are told quite a lot about where Sipho lives. What can we **infer** about his life from this information?

6 Copy and complete the table below, adding your own ideas to all three columns. Return to your answer to question 1 to help fill in column 1.

Reference	Where	What we can infer
'A small square of plastic above the bed let in the dim early morning light'	Paragraph 1	No proper windows in the house
'…the orange-crate cupboard'	Paragraph 1	
'Shop boarded up overnight…'		
'Bullets whistling…'		

Exploring further: Adding impact

7 a) In paragraph 2, Naidoo uses two similes to describe Sipho. Identify them and note down what they tell us about Sipho's feelings.

b) A metaphor is used for less powerful description when the writer describes the 'patchwork of shacks' that Sipho passes through. What qualities are suggested by this description?

Focus on: Adding quotations to your writing

When you are writing about texts, either in class or in a test situation, you need to provide evidence for what you write. So, using the table on page 153, we could write:

> The writer tells us that Sipho's home has a 'small square of plastic above the bed'. This suggests that Sipho's house does not have proper windows and that his family is poor.

Notice that the actual words (**quotation**) from the text have **inverted commas** around them. Also note that the writer finishes by telling us what we can infer from this quotation.

8 Practise using quotations properly in these two examples. You will need to:
- find a suitable quotation from the text
- add it to the sentence and insert inverted commas in the correct place.

a) We can tell that Sipho is worried that the door will make a noise because he mentions its…

b) It is clear that Sipho's stepfather is very large because he is described as…

Exploring further: Editing quotations

In the example at the top of the page, the quotation has been carefully included as part of the sentence:

9 Look at the information below and the two methods of using quotations. Which do you think is the more fluent method of linking the point and the quotation together?

- **Point:** Sipho is pretty inexperienced at travelling.
- **Quotation:** 'With so many taxis, he had to make sure he got in the right one'.

A Sipho is a pretty inexperienced traveller, as he says: 'With so many taxis, he had to make sure he got in the right one'.

B Because there were 'so many taxis', Sipho needed to make sure he 'got in the right one', thus showing he is a pretty inexperienced traveller.

Key Writing

R1

10 a) Check through the second half of text to find any references to buildings or the setting. Add these to the table you started for question 6.

Make sure you decide what you infer from each detail. For example, don't just say that Sipho doesn't have proper windows.

b) Write three paragraphs about what we find out about Sipho's home and the area he lives in. Paragraph 1 should be about his home, paragraph 2 should be about his neighbourhood and paragraph 3 should sum up the overall view presented of the setting. Refer back to your work in question 1 if necessary.

You could start them like this, or use your own structure if you prefer:

Paragraph 1: Sipho's home is…

Paragraph 2: His home is situated in a…

Paragraph 3: The general impression given is…

Remember to:
- support what you say with quotations
- put the quotations inside inverted commas (speech marks)
- edit the quotation (cut out bits that don't fit or are not relevant).

11 Scan the text for references to Sipho's stepfather and his mother, and then make very brief notes saying what impression we get of both of them from what we are told.

For example:
- Stepfather: Paragraph 1: large – 'giant of a man'
- Mother: Paragraph 1: pregnant – 'rounded stomach'

3 Tiger tracking in Rajasthan

Aims

- Read an information text about tigers in Rajasthan, India
- Look at how to adjust your style to suit purpose and audience
- Explore how writers bring together different types of information (Wr9)
- Write an information text for a different audience (S9)

In this extract about another land, the tiger takes centre stage. But man's influence is never far away…

Lying 109 miles (176 km) southwest of Bharatpur, near the town of Sawai Madhopur and at the junction of the Aravalli and Viiidhya ranges, Ranthambore National Park is one of the best places in the world to see tigers in the wild. This 198 square mile (513 km^2) park, once the private hunting grounds of the maharajas of Jaipur, became a national park in 1973 as part of Project Tiger. The road into the park winds through a steep desert canyon opening onto a region of marshes, streams, lakes, grasslands and craggy hills. Much of the area is covered by virgin deciduous forests studded with palms. Mango groves and huge banyans grow around the lakes.

On drives in open-sided jeeps, you'll see abundant wildlife, including sambars (large deer), Indian gazelles, langur monkeys, blue bucks, sloth bears, marsh crocodiles and Indian flying foxes. The tigers are elusive, and sightings can never be guaranteed, but, with luck, you may experience the thrill of seeing a tigress with her young as you wind through the forest in the early morning or late afternoon. You'll certainly see a wide range of birds, including paradise flycatchers, green pigeons, pheasant-tailed jaçanas, white wagtails, and even crested serpent eagles.

Jogi Mahal, the former hunting lodge of the maharajas, overlooks the main marsh, Padam Talao, where painted storks and spotted deer feed. At night here, you may hear the scream of a leopard or the hoot of an eagle owl. The massive Ranthambore

Fort, built in the tenth century and located on a ridge-top in the park's southwestern corner, affords a spectacular panoramic view. Throughout the park you'll see remnants of the past: pavilions, tombs and hunting blinds. Allow at least three days here in order to make the most of your visit.

India's national parks are islands of native habitat in a country where the pressures of population are making ever-growing demands for farming land. Remarkably, over 300 parks covering 35,000 square miles (90,000 km^2) have been set aside to protect endangered species and habitats. There have, however, been significant disputes, and unless India's population growth is curbed, the demand for food may become too great to save these preserves.

In 1973, Project Tiger was launched in India to protect and rehabilitate tiger populations in nine sanctuaries and national parks with a variety of habitats. Hunting these magnificent cats has been banned since that time and, as a result, tiger numbers have increased from 1,800 to about 4,000.

There are now eight tiger preserves throughout the country. Much has been learned about tigers by biologists, particularly in Ranthambore, where the tigers are thriving under protection; tigers here are no longer afraid of humans and are often seen padding about in broad daylight. Previously it was thought that they were strictly nocturnal. Project Tiger has saved tigers from extinction, but corruption in local management, poaching, and pressures for timber and grazing land pose major threats to their habitat, particularly in times of drought.

Key Reading

Information texts

This text is an **information** text. Its **purpose** is to provide information in order to help us understand a place and some related issues.

The main features of this text are:

- It has an introduction with a **general statement**, followed by logical sections with **specific facts**. For example, the first paragraph mentions the name of the park, and that it is 'one of the best places in the world to see tigers in the wild'.

- It uses the **present tense** to describe how things are, for example, 'Mango groves and huge banyans *grow* around the lakes.'

- It uses **formal** and **impersonal language**, for example, 'The massive Ranthambore Fort, built in the tenth century and located on a ridge-top in the park's southwestern corner, affords a spectacular panoramic view.'

- It uses **technical** or subject-related **language**, for example: 'tiger populations', 'sanctuaries', 'a variety of habitats'.

1. List as many geographical terms and references as you can from paragraph 1. Why do you think there are so many?

2. Although the present tense is used to tell us current information, other verb tenses are also used. For example:

> Remarkably, over 300 parks covering 35,000 square miles (90,000 km^2) have been set aside to protect endangered species and habitats.
>
> On drives in open-sided jeeps, you'll see abundant wildlife, including sambars (a large deer)…

a) Name the two different tenses in these examples.
b) Why has each of these tenses been used?

3 Identify the words and phrases in this short extract that make the language both formal and impersonal:

> There have, however, been significant disputes, and unless India's population growth is curbed…

Purpose

On the surface this seems to be purely an information text. It tells us about the national park and the creatures that can be seen there. But is there a message behind this information?

4 Reread the final two paragraphs and discuss these questions in pairs:

　a) What viewpoint or opinion do you think we are given about tigers and their situation from these paragraphs?

　b) Which key words or phrases suggest this?

A tiger being tagged

Reading for meaning

5 Although this is an information text, the writer does make it sound as if Ranthambore is a place worth visiting.

> On drives in open-sided jeeps, you'll see abundant wildlife…

> …sightings can never be guaranteed, but, with luck, you may experience the thrill of seeing a tigress with her young as you wind through the forest in the early morning or late afternoon.

a) Which words or phrases suggest a trip to the park will be worthwhile?

b) Can you find a phrase in paragraph 3 that suggests the reader might well plan a trip there?

6 The writer adds a wealth of detail about the park by giving specific facts. In particular he uses lists to show the wide range of geographical, animal and bird life the park holds.

a) Identify three of these lists in paragraphs 1 and 2.

b) What effect would these have on a reader thinking of visiting the park?

Exploring further: The senses

7 a) Look again at paragraph 3. Which two senses does the writer appeal to in particular?

b) Note down an example from paragraph 3 of words or a phrase that appeal to each sense.

c) What is the overall effect created by these descriptions?

Focus on: Bringing together different types of information

The first paragraph of the text provides clear factual information:

> This [size: 198 square mile (513 km²)] park, once the [what it is and who owned it: private hunting grounds of the maharajas of Jaipur], became a [its history/background: national park in 1973]…

However, if the text was just factual information using mostly dates and figures, it would be a bit limited. So the writer also provides us with information we can *visualise* (see in our minds):

> The road into the park winds through a steep desert canyon opening onto a region of marshes, streams, lakes, grasslands and craggy hills.

8 Here is another set of information from the same book but about another national park.

Sort the bullet points into **two** lists:
- List 1, which provides mostly figures and dates
- List 2, which provides information that creates an image in our minds.

A Bharatpur, one of Rajasthan's four national parks
B Consists of lakes and canals fed by local rivers
C Located 33 miles west of Agra
D Shallow marshes provide wintering sites for birds
E 11 square miles (29 km²) in area
F Large thorny acacia trees line the paths
G 350 species of birds
H 41 miles (66 km) of trails
I World-famous heron sanctuary where 30,000 chicks born each year
J Once the duck hunting preserve of the maharajahs of Bharatpur
K Forest around marshes has deciduous, scrub and thorn trees
L At night-time haunting calls of jackals, stone-curlews and seven species of owl can be heard

Tiger tracking in Rajasthan

Key Writing

9 Take this information from lists 1 and 2 and turn it into a two-paragraph information text.

Decide what each paragraph will focus on (i.e. the facts and figures or the images/sounds of the landscape) and then draft them. You will need to turn the lettered points from notes into full sentences by:

- adding or changing words
- using link words or phrases between the sentences (connectives, conjunctions or sentence signposts such as 'and', 'where', 'in the midst of the forests…').

For example:

> Bharatpur **is** one of Rajasthan's four national parks, **and**…

added word to make a sentence

conjunction links to next bit of information

10 Now rewrite the same information for younger children.
- You will need to replace or remove several words (for example, 'located', 'consist of', 'provide').
- You may need to explain other words.
- You may decide to create shorter, simpler paragraphs.
- You may want to introduce a subheading above each paragraph.

Exploring further: Text boxes

Information texts like these often feature separate text boxes to provide explanations or further information.

11 a) Choose two of the following topics and do some basic research.
- maharajahs
- poaching
- mahals
- flying foxes
- deciduous trees.

b) Create a simple box of bullet points on each topic to add to the article, for example:

> **Maharajas**
> - From Hindi words meaning 'great' and 'king'.
> •

④ Unit 7 Assignment: Himalaya correspondent

Assessment Focus

▸ AF3 Organise and present whole texts effectively, sequencing and structuring information, ideas and events

> **You:** are a journalist who writes articles for a magazine about remote places and people.
> **Your task:** to write about the Himalayas and threats to the environment.

Stage 1

Below and on page 164 are the notes you made during your research:

- Himalayas: more than 1,600 miles (2,600 km) in size from west to east
- Some countries they go through: Pakistan, India, Tibet, Nepal and Bhutan
- The Great Himalaya chain in Nepal and Tibet has highest mountains, with Mount Everest at 29,028 feet (8,854m) being the highest
- Sherpas (local guides) very skilled – means rich and inexperienced climbers can even get to top of peaks like Everest
- Lots of rubbish along the trails – the worst being at the top of Everest
- 200,000 tourists visit Nepal each year
- Hillsides are eroding because firewood needed to keep trekkers and porters warm
- 77,000 trekking permits issued each year

- Nepalese businessman plans to open a cyber-café halfway up Everest
- Most animals seen tend to be domestic ones – yaks, goats and chickens
- Sometimes Langur monkeys, monal pheasants can be seen on lower forest trails
- Higher up – golden eagles and elusive snow leopards might be seen
- Some group treks now come just to clean up rubbish on trails

Sort these points into two lists:
- List 1 is mainly concerned with facts and figures
- List 2 is concerned with what can be seen and the problems and other issues.

Stage 2

Decide on a title for your article. Then organise your two lists into four paragraphs. You could follow this structure:

Paragraph 1: Information about the Himalayas, where they are, etc.
Paragraph 2: Information about the number of travellers, walkers, trekkers
Paragraph 3: The wildlife that can be seen
Paragraph 4: Problems and issues.

You could, however, follow your own structure, provided there is a focus for each paragraph.

Stage 3

Draft your information text, using your plan as a guide.

- Use connectives, conjunctions or sentence signposts to link your ideas and say as much as you can.
- Think carefully about the formality of the language: although this text will present some of the problems about the Himalayas, this is not a personal piece, so do not use the first person ('I'). Model your work on the style of the text on pages 156–157.
- Use the present tense.
- Include technical terms where they help to present information.

Stage 4

- Access some images of the Himalayas on the Internet or in your school library to illustrate your article. Add some captions to the images (short descriptions that go underneath). Lay out your text and images together as one article.

Challenge

Add three text boxes that feature added information about:
- the sherpas
- golden eagles
- other facts about Everest.

Add these to your article to create a complete informative article. As you do so, consider other ways of making it appealing and informative (for example, icons, subheadings, different fonts).

Unit 8 Darkness visible

1 The salt marshes

Aims

- Read an extract from *The Woman in Black*
- Learn to identify different layers of meaning in a text and to identify mood (W7)
- Learn how paragraphs can be developed as well as linked (S6)
- Consider the reader's point of view
- Discuss the role of the narrator
- Write a ghost story

This extract comes from *The Woman in Black* by Susan Hill. Arthur Kipps, a solicitor, is returning from the funeral of Mrs Alice Drablow. Her house – Eel Marsh House – looks out on the lonely and dangerous salt marshes and is linked to the mainland by Nine Lives Causeway.

On the causeway path it was still quite dry underfoot but to my left I saw that the water had begun to seep nearer, quite silent now, quite slow. I wondered how deeply the path went under water when the tide was at its height. But on a still night such as this, there was plenty of time to cross in safety, though the
5   distance was greater, now I was traversing it on foot, than it had seemed when we trotted over in Keckwick's pony cart, and the end of the causeway path seemed to be receding into the greyness ahead. I had never been quite so alone, nor felt quite so small and insignificant in a vast landscape before, and I fell into a not unpleasant brooding, philosophical frame of mind, struck by the
10 absolute indifference of water and sky to my presence.

   Some minutes later, I could not tell how many, I came out of my reverie, to realize that I could no longer see very far in front of me and when I turned around I was startled to find that Eel Marsh House, too, was invisible, not because the darkness of evening had fallen, but because of a thick, damp sea-
15 mist that had come rolling over the marshes and enveloped everything, myself, the house behind me, the end of the causeway path and the countryside ahead. It was a mist like a damp clinging cobwebby thing, fine and yet impenetrable…I felt confused, teased by it, as though it were made up of

20 millions of live fingers that crept over me, hung on me and then shifted away again. Above all, it was the suddenness of it that had so unnerved and disorientated me.

For a short time, I walked slowly on, determined to stick to my path until I came out onto the safety of the country road. But it began to dawn upon me that I should as likely as not become very quickly lost once I had left the
25 straightness of the causeway, and might wander all night in exhaustion. The most obvious and sensible course was to turn and retrace my steps the few hundred yards I had come and to wait at the house until either the mist cleared or Keckwick arrived to fetch me, or both.

That walk back was a nightmare. I was obliged to go step by slow step, for fear
30 of veering off onto the marsh, and then into the rising water. If I looked up or around me, I was at once baffled by the moving, shifting mist, and so on I stumbled, praying to reach the house, which was farther away than I had imagined. Then somewhere away in the swirling mist and dark, I heard the sound that lifted my heart, the distant but unmistakable clip-clop of the pony's
35 hooves and the rumble and creak of the trap. So Keckwick was unperturbed by the mist, quite used to travelling through the lanes and across the causeway in darkness, and I stopped and waited to see a lantern – for surely he must carry one – and half wondered whether to shout and make my presence known, in case he came suddenly upon me and ran me down into the ditch.

40 Then I realised that the mist played tricks with sound as well as sight, for not only did the noise of the trap stay further away from me for longer than I might have expected but also it seemed to come not from directly behind me, straight down the causeway path, but instead to be away to my right, out on the marsh. I tried to work out the direction of the wind but there was none. I turned
45 around but then the sound began to recede further away again. Baffled, I stood and waited, straining to listen through the mist. What I heard next chilled and horrified me, even though I could neither understand nor account for it. The noise of the pony trap grew fainter then stopped abruptly and away on the marsh was a curious draining, sucking, churning sound, which went on,
50 together with the shrill neighing and whinnying of a horse in panic, and then I heard another cry, a shout, a terrified sobbing – it was hard to decipher – but with horror I realized that it came from a child, a young child. I stood absolutely helpless in the mist that clouded me and everything from my sight, almost weeping in an agony of fear and frustration, and I knew that I was
55 hearing, beyond any doubt, appalling last noises of a pony and trap, carrying a child in it, as well as whatever adult – presumably Keckwick – was driving and was even now struggling desperately. It had somehow lost the causeway path and fallen into the marshes and was being dragged under by the quicksand and the pull of the incoming tide.

60 I began to yell until I thought my lungs would burst…

Darkness visible

Key Reading

> **Narrative texts**
>
> This text is a story or **narrative**. The **purpose** of a narrative is to entertain us.
>
> The main features of this text are:
>
> - It has a structure that includes an **introduction**, a problem or **complication**, a **crisis** and a **resolution** when things are sorted out. The opening of a text may introduce a setting, an event or a character.
>
> - It has a **narrator** – who in this case tells the story in the first person (I), for example, '*I* was obliged to go step by slow step…'
>
> - It uses **powerful and descriptive language** to maintain the interest of the reader, for example, 'I was *startled* to find that Eel Marsh House, too, was *invisible*…'

1 Identify two features in paragraph 1 that suggest the extract comes from a Gothic novel (a narrative dealing with frightening or supernatural events).

2 **a)** Find evidence that this extract is written in the first person.

   b) Who is the narrator, and what position does he have in the story?

3 Does this extract come from the beginning, middle or the end of the novel? How can you tell?

4 Over what length of time do you think the events take place?

5 What mood do the words in italics create in the example below?

> I was *startled* to find that Eel Marsh House, too, was *invisible*…

Purpose

6 a) *The Woman in Black* was first published in 1983. Why is this significant? Is it surprising?

  b) Why do you think the writer wrote the story? Think of two reasons, taking into account your answer to question 1.

7 a) At the end of the extract, what two things do you most want to find out?

  b) Why does the final line make the reader want to read on?

> **infer** work out or deduce a meaning
> **imply** suggest or hint at a meaning that is not obvious

Reading for meaning

When we begin reading the extract we quickly gain a sense that something unfortunate might happen.

8 a) Study the first sentence. Where is Arthur when the extract opens? Find the exact words that tell you, and explain what they mean. Use a dictionary if you need to.

  b) Now study the final words of the sentence: 'quite silent now, quite slow'.

  What do you infer from these words about the landscape and about Arthur's situation?

The salt marshes

9 a) Near the beginning of paragraph 2, what else happens to make Arthur's situation worse?

b) Something deeper is also implied in paragraph 2. What would you expect this to be in a Gothic novel? Find the relevant part of the description and study the language closely.

c) Now write a short paragraph saying what you think could be threatening Arthur. Explore at least two possibilities.

Exploring further: The reader's point of view

During this opening, the reader forms an opinion of Arthur as events unfold.

10 a) Read paragraph 1 again. How does Arthur feel at this point about crossing the causeway? Find the exact words that tell you.

b) How does the reader view Arthur's attitude? What does the last sentence of paragraph 1 tell you about him?

c) Look through the extract and find other evidence of Arthur's character traits. Use it to write a short character sketch.

Focus on: The mood

The mood or **tone** of a piece of writing is the kind of feeling created. When tension is building up in a story, new paragraphs often signal an increase in mood or shifts of mood, as well as giving information. This is true in this extract.

11 a) Look back at paragraph 1. Here we could say that the mood created is one of concern. Now look at paragraph 2. In this paragraph concern has become anxiety.

Which words in paragraph 2 help to suggest this?

b) Draw up a table like the one below. In pairs, write in column 1 the first sentence (or the sentence signpost) in each paragraph, that shows the key idea.

Sentence signpost	Mood created
Paragraph 1: 'On the causeway path it was still quite dry underfoot but to my left I saw that the water had begun to seep nearer...'	concern – something unfortunate could happen

c) Next, discuss what kind of mood is created in each paragraph and why. Note any build-up in tension or shift of mood. Record your thoughts in column 2 of your table. Try to find words that describe the mood as accurately as possible. Use a thesaurus to help you.

Exploring further: Developing paragraphs

Connectives are often used to develop paragraphs, as well as to open them.

12 a) Look back at your table from question 11 and the sentence signpost you recorded for paragraph 3. What connective does it begin with?

b) What connective starts the next sentence in the paragraph? What change of mood does it help to indicate?

Exploring further: The unreliable narrator

Usually when we read a text we trust what the narrator is telling us. An **unreliable narrator** is a narrator the reader cannot be sure of. For example, a story in which the narrator has limited information might cause the reader to wonder where the fictional truth lies. A narrator may also be reliable at one point in the story and not at another.

13 a) In pairs, discuss what appears to have happened by the end of the extract and who is involved. Look closely at the text for evidence that the events may still be unclear.

b) What do you think might really have happened? Think of several possibilities.

Key Writing

14 Imagine you are Arthur, looking back many years later at the events in the extract. Several people are listening to you around the fireside at the local inn. Keckwick is one of them.

Write about the events on the causeway, taking these questions into account:
- Who was in the carriage?
- What happened to it?
- How was Keckwick involved?
- What happened to you (as Arthur) and what did you do?
- Are you as the narrator certain of events or not?

Remember to:
- narrate the tale in the first person, using the past tense
- link and develop your paragraphs using sentence signposts to build up tension and to signal changes of mood
- include sentences where the reader must try to infer a deeper meaning, but cannot be sure
- use powerful verbs, nouns, adjectives and adverbs in your descriptions in the style of the original extract.

② Fears and phobias

Aims

- Read an information text about fears and phobias
- Examine the layout features of a text and how and why you might change them (Wr4)
- Study an example that is used to explain a point and write your own example
- Study how modal verbs help us to explore possibilities
- Redraft an information text

This webpage is taken from a self-help health website.

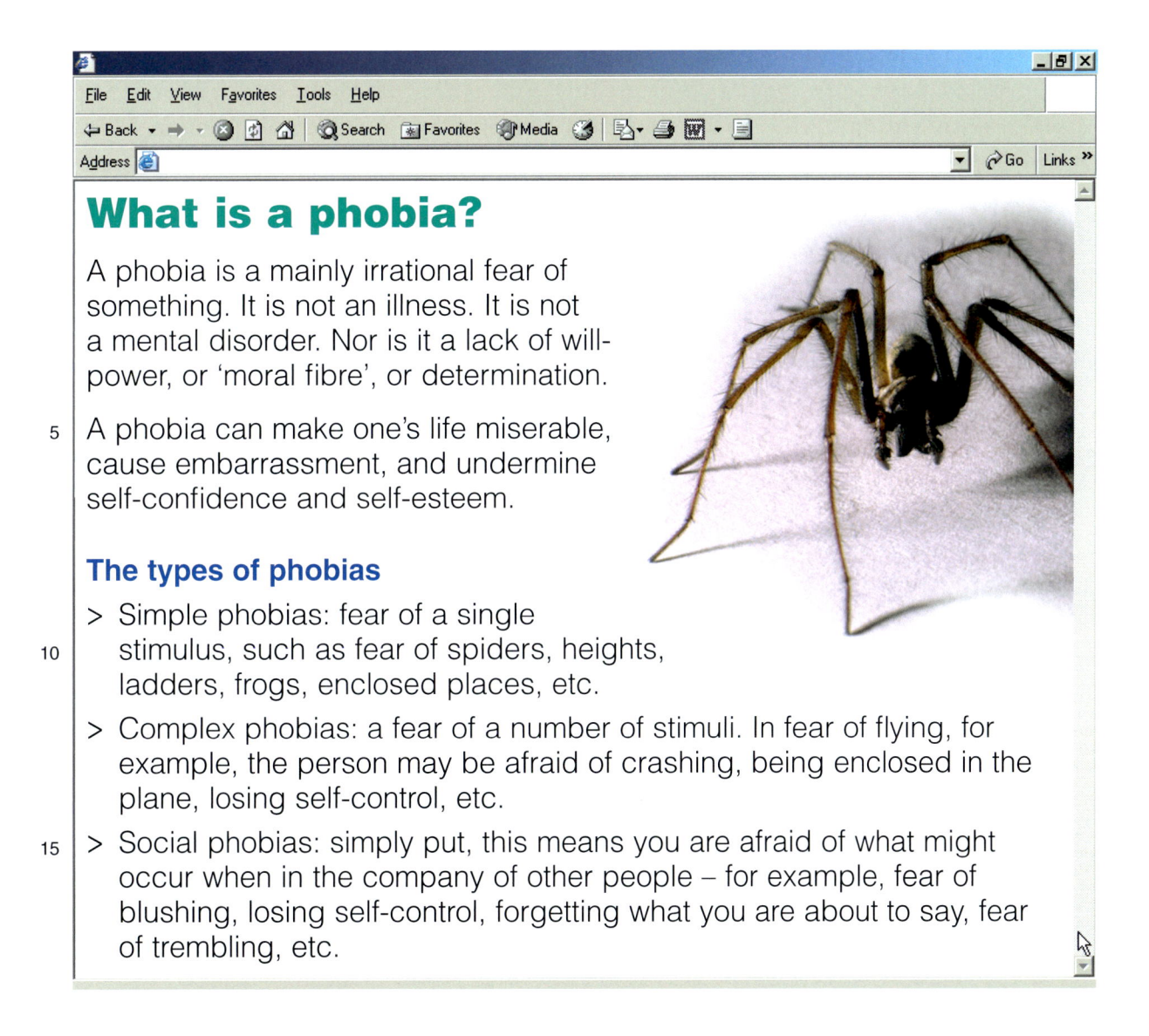

What is a phobia?

A phobia is a mainly irrational fear of something. It is not an illness. It is not a mental disorder. Nor is it a lack of will-power, or 'moral fibre', or determination.

5   A phobia can make one's life miserable, cause embarrassment, and undermine self-confidence and self-esteem.

The types of phobias

> Simple phobias: fear of a single
10   stimulus, such as fear of spiders, heights, ladders, frogs, enclosed places, etc.

> Complex phobias: a fear of a number of stimuli. In fear of flying, for example, the person may be afraid of crashing, being enclosed in the plane, losing self-control, etc.

15 > Social phobias: simply put, this means you are afraid of what might occur when in the company of other people – for example, fear of blushing, losing self-control, forgetting what you are about to say, fear of trembling, etc.

> Panic attacks: a panic attack can be quite a terrifying ordeal unless you understand what is going on and why it is going on. Panic attacks are very common and appear mainly to affect people who normally give the impression of being confident, reliable and dependable.

> Agoraphobia: Literally 'fear of the market place' and, up to a decade or so ago, the term was used to describe people who were afraid of open spaces. 'Agoraphobia' is now used to describe those who experience increasing nervousness the further they travel from their own home. In severe cases they may not venture from home at all.

The difference between a fear and a phobia

The distinction generally made is to say that a fear is rational and that when fear becomes irrational it is a phobia.

In reality the difference is mainly one of degree and the handiest way to distinguish them is by saying that a phobia is different from a fear by being more irrational. Because, having being fuelled by our imagination, every fear will have a degree of irrationality to it.

Irrational fear

A phobia is an irrational fear – which is why someone who is phobic will often say 'I know it's silly, but…' They are quite well aware that, while there may be some rational basis for their fear, it is largely irrational.

Take the example of a phobia of snakes. If you live in the United Kingdom there is a slight possibility that you may be out in the countryside on a warm summer's day and you may possibly come across one of our increasingly rare adders, and you just might not see it, and it might be so unaware of your very silent approach that it doesn't quietly slip away, and you might possibly be walking about without wearing shoes, and you might possibly step on it and get bitten.

All of this is not very likely, I agree, but it is just possible. And therefore a UK resident has some reason to be fearful of snakes.

Yet, while the likelihood of being bitten by an adder in the UK is very small, someone who is afraid of snakes can be so fearful that they cannot even pass a pet shop just in case there may be snakes on display in the window. They may even have to leave the room if snakes are featured on the television. Or be unable to look at a picture of snakes in a magazine.

Key Reading

> ### Information texts
>
> This text is mainly an **information** text. Its **purpose** is to give clear information about a topic.
>
> The main features of this text are:
> - It uses the **present tense** when it is telling things as they are, for example, 'A phobia *is* a mainly irrational fear…'
> - Its **layout** includes **headings and subheadings** to make it easier to find information and allow the reader to browse, for example: 'The types of phobias'.
> - It includes **technical language** related to the topic, for example: 'complex phobias', 'social phobias', 'agorophobia'.
> - It contains a **general statement** that introduces the topic, followed by **specific facts**.

1 a) What two important points are made about phobias in the opening statement?

b) What does a lack of 'moral fibre' mean?

c) The opening statement also discusses the things that a phobia is 'not'. What are these?

d) What different types of phobias are covered?

2 a) From what point of view (in what 'person') is the text mainly written?

b) What other points of view ('persons') are also included?

Purpose

3 a) You can see at a glance what the author's main concern is in this text. How does the layout help to make this clear? What is this main concern?

b) What other purposes does the text have?

4 a) Most information texts are written in a formal style, but this one has a chatty style in many paragraphs. Find an example of each.

b) Why do you think this text includes both styles?

c) Who would be the main audience for this text? What other groups might also be interested in reading it?

Reading for meaning

The layout of the text includes subheadings, meaning the reader can browse the text – paying attention to some parts and ignoring others. However, under each subheading the paragraphs can contain a great deal of information.

5 In a small group, you are going to work out how you could add to or change the layout of the text to make it:

- easier to find information
- look more attractive.

a) First, look through the whole text from the opening statement to the final paragraph.
 – Share ideas and discuss their usefulness.
 – Reject some ideas and retain others.

b) Choose someone to record at least four points of your group's best ideas. Be ready to feed back to the class and keep any notes you make for later tasks.

Grammar for reading

Colons can introduce a list or indicate who is about to speak in a script.

Single quotation marks are used around titles such as book titles, when quoting from another text or to emphasise an expression.

Ellipses (…) show that words have been omitted in a quotation.

Exploring further: Use of punctuation

The text uses a range of punctuation for different purposes. The uses of each of these are detailed on page 176.

6 a) Find examples of colons and quotation marks under the subheading 'The types of phobias', and decide why they have been used.

b) Why are commas also important in this section?

c) Under the subheading 'Irrational fear', a dash and an ellipsis have been used in the same sentence. What is the function of each of these?

Focus on: Making a point clear

7 Reread the paragraphs of the extract under the subheading 'Irrational fear'. In the first of these paragraphs an example is given. It runs through the example like a story, using modal verbs to suggest what might happen. The example is also written in the second person singular.

a) Identify the modal verbs this example contains.

b) Why do you think it is told as a narrative?

8 Decide what point is being made in the final two paragraphs.

Grammar for reading

Modal verbs, such as 'should', 'would', 'could', 'might' and 'may', help us to think about the likelihood of different possibilities. They also show that an action depends on something else for it to happen, for example: 'I could see the film if…'

Darkness visible

Exploring further

9 Refer back to the information in the extract on panic attacks. In addition, read the following passage:

> During these attacks there are physical changes in the body so that the heart beats faster and there is sweating. These are also symptoms of anxiety, but during panic attacks the condition is much worse. Breathing is rapid and people can hyperventilate (overbreathe). In addition there are also a sense of impending doom and fears of death.

Explain in writing the difference between a panic attack and a normal level of anxiety.

- Use a narrative style.
- Write in the second-person singular ('you').
- Follow the example in lines 39–45 as your model. Remember, you are attempting to explain the difference between one thing and another using a narrative style.

Key Writing

10 Redraft the text *What is a phobia?* and present it in a user-friendly way.

To do this you will need to:

- cut back the information in each subsection, while making sure you keep the correct definitions and give examples
- use simpler, more informal language
- include useful punctuation to add clarity of information.

For example, you could replace:

> **Simple Phobias:** fear of *a single stimulus* such as fear of spiders, heights, frogs, enclosed places, etc.

with:

> **Simple Phobias:** fear of one thing, such as fear of heights or ladders.

Then use the layout features you devised in question 5. You may need to alter these in light of what you have written.

3 To Kill a Mockingbird

Aims

- Read an extract from the play of *To Kill A Mockingbird* (R14)
- Learn about the importance of stage directions
- Learn how lighting can be used to create atmosphere
- Study the same extract in the novel
- Discuss the differences between the two extracts (R10)

To Kill A Mockingbird is a novel written by Harper Lee and set in the southern states of America during the 1930s. This extract from the play (based on the novel and written by Christopher Sergal), involves Scout Finch and her older brother Jem. The character called Jean is Scout as an adult, looking back and commenting on the action.

(As they go into the house, the light begins to dim except for a small isolated light on JEAN. As she speaks, the light continues to dim until the stage is entirely dark except for her, and she is only dimly seen.)

5 JEAN: Atticus was underestimating what anger and sick frustration could do to an already unbalanced man. The night we found out – there was a pageant at the school auditorium and Jem said that he'd take me. It was to be our longest journey together. Wind was coming up and Jem
10 said it might be raining before we got home. Heavy clouds had blacked out the moon, and it was pitch dark. Before we left, Cal had a pinprick of apprehension. When I asked what was the matter, she said 'Somebody just walked over my grave.' On the way to school, Jem had a flashlight.

15 (At this JEM turns on a pinpoint flashlight, directing it into SCOUT's face.)

	JEM *(teasing)*:	You scared? Scared of haints?
	SCOUT *(scornfully)*:	Haints, hot steams, incantations, secret signs – I'm too old.
20	JEM *(reciting)*:	'Angel bright, life-in-death, get off the road, don't suck my breath.'
	SCOUT *(sharply)*:	Cut it out!
	JEM:	You're scared now because we're passin' Boo Radley's place.
25	SCOUT:	I'm *not* scared. 'Sides he must not be home.
	JEM:	How c'n ya tell?
30	SCOUT *(logically)*:	If he was, there wouldn't be a bird singing in the Radley tree. Hear that mocker?
	(As they listen to the birdsong, the flashlight goes out.)	
	SCOUT:	Turn on the light again.
	JEM:	Something wrong with it. C'mon. Gimme your hand.
35	*(They start to go.)*	
	SCOUT:	How do you know where we're at?
40	JEM:	I can tell we're under the tree now because we're passing through a cool spot. *(As they are going offstage)* Careful.
45 50	JEAN:	The trip back from the pageant was more eventful. The moon had been in and out of the heavy rainclouds, but as we started home it was black dark – and there was the stillness that sometimes comes before a thunderstorm. *(Her voice becoming increasingly involved.)* Jem thought he heard something, and we stopped to listen. Then we walked a few more steps, and he stopped again. I thought he was trying to scare me, but that wasn't it. He held my hand tight and pulled me along fast. Then we stopped suddenly.

55   (There are sounds of several steps being taken, and then they stop.)

JEAN: I thought I heard steps following, too.

(There is a rumble of distant thunder. SCOUT speaks to JEM in the darkness. The light on JEAN has dimmed away.
60 The stage is in total darkness.)

SCOUT *(voice in the darkness)*: Jem, are you afraid?

JEM *(voice)*: Think we're not too far to the tree now.

65 SCOUT: Reckon we ought to sing, Jem.

JEM *(worried)*: No. Be real quiet, Scout.

(There is another rumble of thunder.)

SCOUT: Just the thunderstorm getting closer.

JEM *(more worried)*: No, not that – Listen!

70 (There is the sound of someone running toward them.)

SCOUT *(with sudden alarm)*: I hear! Jem!

JEM *(shouting imperatively)*: He's coming! Run, Scout! Run! Run!

75 SCOUT *(in trouble)*: I tripped! Jem – help me!

JEM: Get away, Scout – Run!

(Then JEM cries out as someone grabs him. There is a sound of struggling. A man's voice is heard – angry, unintelligible.)

80 ATTACKER: Got 'cha – now you'll – damn ya – show 'em.

(There is a crack and JEM screams with pain.)

Characters

Atticus (Finch) – Scout's and Jem's lawyer father
Cal (Calpurnia) – The Finch's black housekeeper
Boo (Arthur) Radley – a neighbour, nervous and withdrawn

Key Reading

Play scripts

This text is a **play script**. Its **purpose** is to provide a written version for those involved in a play's performance and production. It can also be used for classroom study.

The main features of this text are:

- Its **layout**, which includes text divided into scenes, the names of characters on the left (in capitals), and the words of characters following their names.

- It includes **visual information/directions** in italics. These can describe a scene or a character's actions. In this extract the **stage directions** are detailed and sometimes lengthy. They are written in italics within brackets.

- The **dialogue/speech** is not placed within inverted commas. The dialogue often involves short sentences in plays so that it sounds like ordinary speech. (However, Jean's commentary is long because she is giving the audience information.) For example: 'JEM *(more worried)*: No, not that – Listen!'

1 a) Where are the children going to and coming back from? Why is Jem with Scout?

b) What comment spoken by a character in the play and reported by Jean suggests something bad is going to happen?

2 In what way does the weather described in the extract suit the action?

3 Find two stage directions that show a change in Jem's mood.

4 There are many short speeches in the extract. Where do these happen most often? Why?

Purpose

A play tells a story in public and must entertain its **audience**. At the centre of the action there is usually **conflict** between one or more of the characters.

5 a) What is the main conflict in this extract and where does it occur?

b) What other kinds of conflict occur? What is their effect?

6 This play script was adapted with a particular audience in mind. Who do you think the audience might be? Provide a reason for your answer.

7 There are various devices that a playwright can use in a script to support the action on stage. In pairs, refer back to the extract and decide which of these devices are the most important, and why.

Reading for meaning

8 The extract is divided into two short parts or scenes: the first depicts Scout and Jem on their way to the school pageant; the second part depicts the return journey home.

a) In pairs, reread the whole extract to compare with a partner the change of mood and how this is achieved. Consider the following points:

- the nature of Scout's fears in part 1 and part 2 (describe the difference between these fears as accurately as you can)
- Jem's role in parts 1 and 2
- the stage directions
- Jean's commentary.

b) You should each make notes of your findings.

9 Use your notes to write a paragraph (about 150 words) comparing the two scenes. Refer to examples from the script to support your main points and use quotation marks correctly.

Exploring further: Lighting and props

The lighting plays an important part in the extract:
- it creates an atmosphere of tension
- it highlights the characters.

10 a) In a small group, study the stage directions carefully for either the journey to the pageant or the journey back. You will need to decide as a group which journey you will study.

b) Plan how you would use the lighting on stage. To do this:
- follow the stage directions
- follow the children's 'journey' across the stage
- consider where other characters might stand or props be placed and how the lighting affects them.

Draw a series of pictograms (like a storyboard) to show the use of lighting.

Exploring further: Jean's commentary

Jean, as the adult Scout, provides a commentary on the action and adds another layer of meaning. Hers is an authorial voice reflecting on the past.

This technique is a **dramatic device**. In some plays the voice can be off-stage, suggesting a life outside the play or an event taking place elsewhere – for example, in another room.

11 In pairs, discuss other possible ways of presenting or including an off-stage voice. Try to think of examples (such as Shakespeare's plays or Greek tragedy).

Focus on: From novel to play

R10 **12** Below is an extract from the novel of Scout and Jem's return from the pageant.

a) Before studying the annotations, read it through and then find the part in the play script where this scene occurs.

b) The annotations show a few of the similarities and differences between the novel and play script. In pairs, discuss what other differences you can find. Consider:

- what in the play replaces the narrator in the novel
- how the plot or action is conveyed in both texts
- what in the play is used in place of the descriptive passages in the novel.

dialogue very similar to the script — *begins a detailed description of the journey home*

> 'You reckon we oughta sing, Jem?'
> 'No. be real quiet again, Scout.'
> We had not increased our pace. Jem knew as well as I that it was difficult to walk fast without stumping a toe, tripping on stones, and other inconveniences, and I was barefooted. Maybe it was the wind rustling the trees. But there wasn't any wind and there wasn't any trees except the big oak.
> Our company shuffled and dragged his feet, as if wearing heavy shoes. Whoever it was wore thick cotton pants; what I thought were trees rustling was the soft swish of cotton on cotton, wheek, wheek, with every step.
> I felt the sand go cold under my feet and I knew we were near the big oak. Jem pressed my head. We stopped and listened.
> Shuffle-foot had not stopped with us this time. His trousers swished softly and steadily. Then they stopped. He was running, running towards us with no child's steps.
> 'Run, Scout! Run! Run!' Jem screamed.

weather different in the play — *begins a detailed description of the attacker*

To Kill a Mockingbird

185

Key Speaking and Listening

13 a) In a group of four, discuss the following questions:
- After reading the extract from the novel, why do you think stage directions are important in the script?
- How would you play Scout's part from your reading of the script?
- What changes would you make to the way you might play Scout's part after reading the extract from the novel?
- From your readings of the novel and the script, how would you play Jem?
- How should the attacker be played?
- What changes would you make, if any, to Jean's role in the light of the extract from the novel?

b) Rehearse a performance of the scene using the ideas you have explored in your discussion. One of you will need to take control of the sound effects vital to the scene.

Remember to:
- vary your tone to match the stage directions of the script
- use sound effects carefully to create tension.

Exploring further: Reviewing your performance

14 As a group, review how you performed your scene. Focus on one or two areas to improve – for example, Scout's movements (remember: she is barefoot).

④ Unit 8 Assignment: Self-help

Assessment Focuses

◗ AF2 Produce texts which are appropriate to task, reader and purpose
◗ AF5 Vary sentences for clarity, purpose and effect

> **You:** are a writer.
>
> **Your task:** to write a self-help leaflet on fears and how to overcome them. The leaflet is mainly an information text but it also includes advice.

Stage 1

Plan your leaflet using the information provided below.

Paragraph 1
Refer back to pages 173–174 and find the information about what fears are in the webpage text. Look at the subheading: 'The difference between a fear and a phobia'. Focus on gathering information on fears, not phobias. You will draw on this information to write your introduction.

Paragraph 2
Study the notes below. Think of three or four additional examples of stressful situations. Take into account social as well as work situations.

You will need to draw on these notes to write a further paragraph, without including every example. Select the best information.

> **We are under stress in many situations.**
> For example:
> - examinations
> - performing on stage
> - sporting competitions.

Paragraph 3
Next, include a paragraph on how to overcome fears. This time use all the information from the notes on the right and add two or three more points of your own. Create a 'Good Advice' text box summarising five useful tips for overcoming fears.

> **We can help overcome fear:**
> - through relaxation exercises – for example, deep breathing, meditation, slow exercise
> - through confidence building – for example, setting achievable targets.

Add the following elements to your leaflet:
- a commentary saying what the page is about
- the aims of the page
- a summary of the advice it cannot give (such as medical advice).

Then decide where you will place this information and how you will set it out.

Stage 2

Use ICT to plan the layout of your leaflet. Think about:
- headings and subheadings
- font sizes
- positioning of your advice text box.

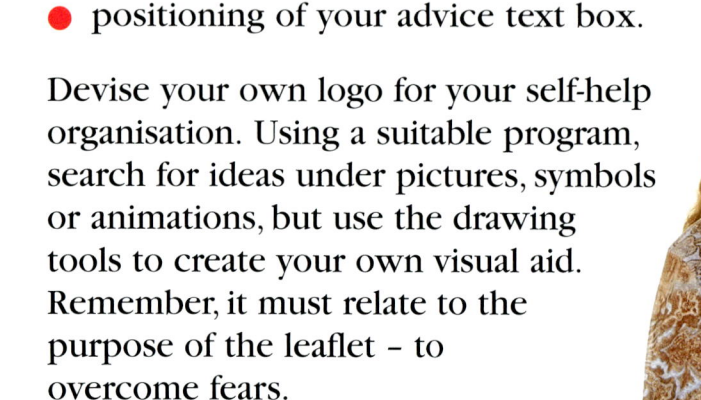

Devise your own logo for your self-help organisation. Using a suitable program, search for ideas under pictures, symbols or animations, but use the drawing tools to create your own visual aid. Remember, it must relate to the purpose of the leaflet – to overcome fears.

Stage 3

Write and set out your leaflet using ICT. Consider these points:
- use the present tense for presenting things as they are
- use an informal, chatty tone
- explain any unfamiliar or technical terms you include
- use imperative verbs in your advice box (for example, 'Make sure…' 'Try to…').

Remember to use a range of ICT tools.

Challenge

Include a case study in your leaflet, using the information below. Decide on a suitable style in which to write it. For example, will you use a narrative form or a recount form for this section?

Case study

Millie R. Student, 16 years old

Problem: Examination fears bring on memory loss

Found these techniques useful:
- mnemonics i.e. words that spell the letters of a keyword – for example, '*g*awky *e*lbows *n*eed *r*egular *e*xercise' spells 'genre' (A mnemonic usually creates a vivid picture.)
- word association, i.e. specific words that revive a memory of other words
- visualising, i.e. seeing a series of points as a journey – for example, from room to room in a house
- relaxation exercises.

Check if you need to change the format of your leaflet. For example, could you convert it from a portrait to a landscape page or from a one-page to a two-page leaflet?

Unit 9 Growing pains

1 The phone call

Aims

- Read an extract from *The Lost Boys Appreciation Society*
- Learn about characters that are also narrators (Wr5)
- Learn about contrasts of mood and figures of speech
- Study the organisation of paragraphs
- Write an account from another character's perspective

The following text is an extract from *The Lost Boys Appreciation Society* by Alan Gibbons. Gary is flicking cold baked beans at his older brother John and being generally irritating, while their father is in the loft looking for something for their mother, who is out. Then the phone rings…

Quite how long it had been ringing before I heard it I'm not sure. The house was bedlam that afternoon, all Gary's fault of course. He had just been flicking cold baked beans at me and slipped out of reach as I took a swipe at him.
　Dr-ing.
5　I jerked to attention. I seemed to understand right away that the call was urgent. I went to get up from the table but Gary started calling me names so I took another swipe at him.
　Dr-ing.
　Somehow the tone seemed more insistent, almost shrill.
10　'Give over,' I said. 'Can't you hear the phone ringing?'
　Gary could hear all right but he didn't care. That's the way it is with Gary, he never knows when to stop, he thinks he's Jack the lad, a real funny guy. The truth is he's training to be the world's greatest pillock. In fact, it's the only thing he puts any effort into, his pillockness. He flicked another cold congealed lump of
15　beany gunge in my direction, spattering my new Ellesse top. It had been flawlessly cream and cool until Gary got to work on it. That did it. I finally flipped and sprang at him. I was coming round the corner of the table when I met resistance. My legs suddenly stiffened and stopped working. Before I could do a

thing about it I stumbled, pitched forward and fell flat on my face. Gary had tied my shoelaces together without me noticing! How could he do that? I didn't feel a thing.

'How old *are* you?' I yelled as I rolled over onto my back. 'That's a stupid kid's trick.'

Dr-ing.'

The prolonged ringing was beginning to worry me. Whoever was on the other end wasn't giving up. They were determined to get an answer. Desperate – and in my mind desperation equals importance.

'Gary, will you get that!'

He just laughed. The spectacle of me rolling round like an upturned beetle was clearly far more entertaining than something as mundane as answering the phone. I was still trying to unknot my laces when Dad came stamping downstairs. I heard him pick up the handset.

'Didn't either of you hear it?' he grumbled. 'I was up in the loft trying to find your mum's sewing machine before she gets home. You'd think you could do one little thing for me.'

'I heard it,' I snapped, 'but El Divvo here tied my shoelaces together.'

Dad was still barking at us when someone spoke at the other end.

'You behave yourself, Gary,' said Dad. 'No argument.'

Gary tried to come back with a smart riposte. He has an answer for everything, our Gary. But Dad wasn't in the mood.

'Just shut it!' he yelled.

The caller must have objected at that point because Dad immediately said, 'No, not you.'

There was a moment's hesitation, then a sound like something bursting, imploding, but far away, as though somebody had pulled the plug on the day. I finally undid my laces and walked to the door. It was for all the world as if the air had been completely sucked out of the hallway. Something was wrong. The anger-flash had drained out of Dad's face, replaced by a blank pallor.

Like disbelief –

Like horror – 'Say – that – again.'

His voice trailed away into the half-light, the final word disintegrating into the dusk. Gary had joined me in the doorway. He too had heard the implosion, a sound beyond hearing, almost, a resonance that shuddered through the house, pulling down certainties. I was looking at Dad, trying to make eye contact, but he continued to stare ahead.

'Dad?'

He held up his hand. His Adam's apple was working strangely in his throat as if he were choking noiselessly. I remembered what he had been doing in the loft – looking for Mum's sewing machine.

Hers.

My mum's.

The link was made in my mind. Suddenly, as if it had been whispered into my ear by some evil spirit. I knew exactly what the call was about. I questioned Dad with my eyes but still he wouldn't return the look. I was making a silent plea, begging it not to be bad news, begging it not to be her. Then I watched Dad's hand go to his face and cover his mouth. Time stood still as his eyes shut tight, squeezing away the threatening tears. He refused to let them come. Even then, even at that moment when our lives broke apart, he continued to play the game. Big boys don't cry.

Growing pains

Key Reading

> **Narrative texts**
>
> This text is a story or **narrative**. The **purpose** of a narrative is to entertain us.
>
> The main features of this text are:
>
> - It has a structure that includes an **introduction**, a problem or **complication**, a **crisis** and a **resolution** when things are sorted out. The opening may introduce a setting, a character or an event.
> - It uses **expressive and descriptive language** (powerful verbs, nouns, adjectives and figurative language) to maintain the interest of the reader. It can be comic: '…he's training to be the world's greatest pillock…' or serious: 'I was making a silent plea, begging it not to be bad news…'
> - It has a **narrator** who tells the story in the first person (I) or the third person (he/she/it), for example: '*I* took a swipe at him' (first person).
> - It has clearly drawn **characters**. In this case the narrator is the **main character** but a minor character can also be a narrator.

1 a) Although the story opens with the description of an ordinary day, we can tell it will be an unforgettable one by the use of a particular word in the second sentence. Can you find it?

b) Which verb at the start of paragraph 3 also indicates something odd is about to happen?

2 What range of moods are depicted in the extract? (Consider all the characters' moods.)

3 Why does John think the phone must be answered?

4 a) What tense is the story mainly told in?

b) Why do you think it is told in this tense?

5 In the narrative certain issues and concerns are explored. From reading this extract, what do you think these might be? Find evidence in the text to support your views.

Purpose

Some writers have an audience in mind before they begin writing.

6 Who might be the target audience for this book? Think of more than one group if you can, and state why each would be interested.

7 How is the reader's interest built up throughout the extract? Think of more than one device that is used.

Reading for meaning

John is both the main character and the narrator, so the story is told from his point of view. It is a first-person narration.

In this kind of narration the character is often looking back and telling the events experienced. We gain a clear picture of his or her thoughts and feelings, relating to him or her, or **empathising** with him or her.

8 a) Think about the main event and the emotions displayed in the extract. Why does the story suit a first-person narration?

b) What might be a disadvantage of having the main character as a narrator?

> **narrative** story
> **narrator** who is telling the story
> **narration** how the story is told

Growing pains

9 a) Using evidence from the extract, make some quick notes on John's character. Focus on:
- his attitude to Gary and his father
- his response to the phone ringing and what this tells you about him.

b) Also make notes on his role as the narrator.

c) Use your notes to write a short character sketch of John.

Exploring further: Multiple narration

If a narrative has multiple narrators, the reader will be told the story from more than one perspective, through the eyes of different characters. The is also likely to include time shifts and changes of scene, and often each of the narrators is unaware of at least part of the story.

10 How would the father depict the events in the extract? Think about:
- his mood
- where he is
- what he is doing.

Wr5

•••••••••••••••••••••••••••

Focus on: Contrasts

You may remember that the mood or tone of a piece of writing is the kind of feeling created. In this extract, the mood changes dramatically when the phone is answered. We are alerted to this change by John's perception that something is shockingly wrong. This sense of shock is made 'concrete' through startling images. It almost seems as if we have stepped into another world. For example:

> There was a moment's hesitation, then a sound like something bursting, imploding, but far away, as though somebody had pulled the plug on the day.

vivid image creates a 'concrete' picture in the reader's mind

11 a) In pairs, find three more vivid images in the extract that are similar to those above. Discuss what each image reminds you of. Think of the concrete pictures that come to mind.

b) Write a short paragraph summarising these images and the pictures you connect with them.

Exploring further: Connecting paragraphs

In the first part of the extract the writer organises the paragraphs to create tension – by breaking the main action every so often with the ringing of the phone.

12 a) Look through the text. Then write down your answers to these questions:
- How often does the ringing occur?
- What is happening just before it rings on each occasion?
- How does John react each time it rings?

b) We can also think of the ringing phone as a **metaphor** because it represents something else. What do you think it represents?

Key Writing

13 What John and Gary fear by the end of the extract is never spelled out. It is only implied. Decide what has happened to their mother and write a scene connected with her. Introduce another character who tells the story from their perspective. (For example, it could be the person at the other end of the phone.)

To help you do this, imagine the scene in the extract and your new scene running parallel. The two scenes could connect at the point where Dad answers the phone.

Your scene should be about 600 words long.

Remember to:

- Begin when the phone starts ringing and include its ringing in your account.
- Use a first-person narration and the past tense.
- Introduce a metaphor – something that signifies what has happened.
- Refer back to the points made under 'multiple narration' to help you.

2 The boy next door?

Aims

- Read a discursive text
- Identify the issue and the arguments in the text
- Recognise that some information in the text will be irrelevant
- Learn about the active and passive tenses
- Explore ways of expressing complex shades of meaning
- Carry out group discussion and come to an agreement (S&L9)

Read the following article from a website and see whether or not you are surprised at the comments.

Boys, it seems, are at the top of the agenda again.

I switched on the television the other day to see some expert being interviewed on the crisis of boys' underachievement in school, compared to girls' achievement.

Yes that old chestnut.

5 So I was about to switch off when the speaker suddenly became animated. 'Boys', he announced… 'well…no wonder they underachieve. It's all to do with their hormones.'

Youths of a certain age it seems have a natural tendency towards aggression, lawlessness, antisocial behaviour, non-communication,
10 dislike of authority (that's anyone from the bus driver to the high-court judge) and are emotionally inept. And it's all down to testosterone overload.

Can this be true?

Only when they reach adulthood do they strive for their place in
15 society, he went on. Then apparently antisocial behaviour is useful for fighting your way to the top.

I thought of the boy next door – that mild-mannered, good-natured, articulate teenage boy. Was he really a wolf in sheep's clothing?

20 No. Not according to a second speaker.

Boys are perfectly capable of managing their behaviour. It all depends on the context.

You mean they're just like the rest of us?

But there was more. Boys, it seems, don't really like education. It's
25 boring. It has low status. And if you want to be one of the boys…

Then up popped a clip of half a dozen young men lounging against a wall. They must have been about fourteen or fifteen years old and were being questioned by a roving reporter. How did they see themselves in relation to girls? This was the third group of boys who'd been interviewed; they came from all sorts of backgrounds and they all said the same.

Boys are definitely different from girls. Boys like football. Girls like talk. Boys like a laugh. Girls like talk. Boys like a rumble. Girls like… You get the picture.

They didn't think much of talk. What was it for? Winding people up?

But there were some good things about girls, they said. They were sympathetic. They were sensible. They thought it was important to work and do well in exams. And crucially, they were different from boys.

The reporter was confused. 'So boys don't care about exams?' He was met with blank faces. 'So boys do care about exams?'

'Yeah – course.' All heads nodded.

On a more serious note it seems boys, like girls, do want to achieve academically, but they don't want to be seen as boffins. Some of this has been backed up by research. Experts suggest that boys' views on gender difference are not fixed but 'dependent on the situation boys find themselves in'.

So I suppose if achieving academically really meant you were man of the match…

But can it be as simple as that?

I decided to ask someone else.

What did my football-crazy, inarticulate, moody, morose, fourteen-year-old daughter think about all this?

'Boys? Boys? I mean 'hullo'. They're like so…' She was lost for words.

'They're like…so… "duh!"'

I wonder what the boy next door would say?

Key Reading

> ### Discursive texts
>
> This text is a **discursive** text. Its **purpose** is to present an argument from different points of view.
>
> The main features of this text are:
>
> - It has a **form** that consists of an **opening statement**, a **series of points** on both sides of the issue and **evidence** supporting these points, for example: 'Some of this has been backed up by research.'
> - It has **sentence signposts** or **key words** to signal which side of the issue is being written about. Sometimes sentences are in the form of a question, for example, 'Was he really a wolf in sheep's clothing? No. Not according to a second speaker.'
> - It uses the **present tense**, but the past tense is also used.
> - It uses some formal **language**, for example, '…it seems boys, like girls, do want to achieve academically…'. However **informal language** is also frequently used to engage the reader, for example: 'Yes, that old chestnut.'

1 a) What is the main issue in the text?

b) What are the two arguments put forward in the article?

2 Point to evidence that suggests that not all boys underachieve and not all girls are articulate.

3 Why do you think formal language is used in the text? Find examples to back up your reasons.

4 a) Several tenses are also used in the article. Find examples of each tense

b) Why is each tense used?

5 What different types of evidence are referred to in the text?

Purpose

6 a) What groups of people would be interested in the issues discussed? Why?

b) Do you get the impression that the author supports one argument over another? Find evidence for your view.

Reading for meaning

The **main issue** is not the same as the two arguments in the text. Look back at the answers you gave to question 1. You should have noted that the main issue focuses on boys' underachievement in school.

The **arguments** present reasons for this underachievement.

7 a) Find the first argument by looking for sentence signposts or key words, and locating the paragraph. Record your findings in a table like the one below.

Argument 1	Paragraph	Sentence signpost

b) In pairs, discuss what Argument 1 means and why it might lead boys to underachieve at school. For example:

'Hormones' are related to physical changes in adolescence. This suggests that boys can't help these changes.

The point is backed up by evidence in the text. What is it? Add your own notes to the table under Argument 1 to explain.

c) Then discuss how the evidence relates to boys' underachievement.

8 In the same way, find Argument 2 and the evidence given to back it up. Remember: Argument 2 is opposed to Argument 1. Argument 2 is also more complex, so look carefully for key words or signposts that tell you *why* boys underachieve. For example, discuss what the boys say to the reporter in lines 36–39. Does this support Argument 2 or not?

Exploring further: Judging the evidence

The type of evidence used in a discursive text will vary depending on its purpose. For example, it could be a reference, such as a date, or it could be a comment that reveals an opinion.

When arguments are presented, some pieces of evidence may be more convincing than others.

9 What do you think is the most convincing piece of evidence in the article? Give your reasons.

Exploring further: Redundant information

Sometimes in discursive texts points are made that are not relevant to the argument. This can be called **redundant** information. We can skip over it when looking for the main points.

10 a) Find a paragraph that is included as part of Argument 1 but does not add anything to it.

b) Write a sentence explaining what it does add to the text.

Focus on: Using the passive form

Both the active and passive forms are used in the text. The active 'voice' speaks directly to the reader. The passive 'voice' is more formal and distant. For example:

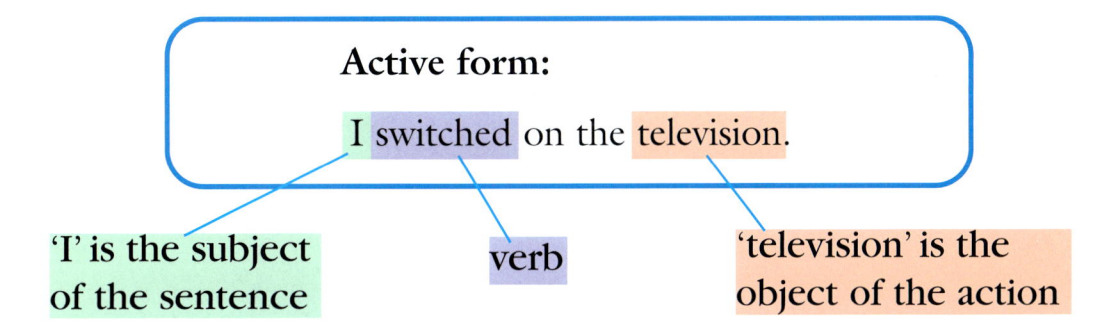

Active form:

I switched on the television.

'I' is the subject of the sentence

verb

'television' is the object of the action

Passive form:

The television was switched on by me.

'television' is the subject

verb

'I' becomes the passive agent of the sentence – 'by me'

In the example above, the agent (or 'by phrase' is included) but in some cases this is left out. For example:

Active form: Scientists conducted experiments.

Passive form: Experiments were conducted.

S3 **11 a)** Explain why the agent is sometimes dropped.

b) Read through the article. Find an example of:
- the active form
- the passive form with an agent
- the passive form without an agent.

Exploring further: Possibility and probability

You will remember that modal verbs (such as 'would', 'should', 'could', 'can' and 'must') help to express more complex shades of meaning. Other verbs and parts of speech also allow us to do this, such as the verb 'suppose'. This helps us to make a comment based on probability.

12 a) Look through the article and find similar parts of speech and expressions. What does each one allow us to do?

b) Techniques such as asking questions are also used. Find examples.

c) These different techniques and parts of speech are useful in discursive texts. Why do you think this is?

Key Speaking and Listening

13 a) Work in a group to discuss the following issues:

- Why do you think boys underachieve in school?
- Why do you think more girls achieve than boys in school?
- Despite the different kinds of achievement by boys and girls, in general men still achieve higher status and greater incomes than women. What do you think the reasons are for this?

- Use the notes you made earlier about Arguments 1 and 2 in the article to start your discussion.
- Develop your ideas by building on each other's points.
- Back up what you say by pointing to evidence and examples.
- Draw on useful points discovered earlier about the arguments and evidence.
- Try to sum up your views as a group. (For example, you could agree on one point of view, neither point of view or think that both views have merit.)

All members of the group should make notes. You will need these to complete the assignment on pages 210–211.

b) Appoint a spokesperson to report your findings to another group. Ask them for feedback. Add any new points to your notes.

3 Chinese Cinderella

Aims

- Read from an autobiography
- Study the use of powerful language (W7)
- Identify the structure of the extract and consider other possible structures
- Study the preface to the autobiography
- Consider the importance of 'memory' in autobiography
- Write a recount from a particular perspective (R6)

The following text is an extract from *Chinese Cinderella* by Adeline Yen Mah. Adeline lives with her father, step-mother and extended family. One evening her father decides to test the obedience of the family dog, Jackie, using Adeline's pet duckling, PLT (Precious Little Treasure).

Father released PLT and placed her in the centre of the lawn. My little pet appeared bewildered by all the commotion. She stood quite still for a few moments, trying to get her bearings: a small, yellow, defenceless creature beset with perils, surrounded by humans wanting to test their dog in a gamble with her life. I sat stiffly with downcast eyes. For a moment, I was unable to focus properly. 'Don't move, PLT! Please don't move!' I prayed silently. 'As long as you keep still, you have a chance!'

Jackie was ordered to 'sit' about two metres away. He sat on his hind legs with his large tongue hanging out, panting away. His fierce eyes were riveted on his prey. Father kept two fingers on his collar while the German Shepherd fidgeted and strained restlessly.

The tension seemed palpable while I hoped against hope that fate could be side-stepped in some way. Then PLT cocked her head in that achingly familiar way of hers and spotted me. Chirping happily, she waddled unsteadily towards me. Tempted beyond endurance, Jackie sprang forward. In one powerful leap, he broke away from Father's restraint and pounced on PLT, who looked up at me pleadingly, as if I was supposed to have an answer to all her terror. Father dashed over, enraged by Jackie's defiance. Immediately, Jackie released the bird from his jaws, but with a pang I saw PLT's left leg dangling lifelessly and her tiny, webbed foot twisted at a grotesque angle. Blood spurted briskly from an open wound.

I was overwhelmed with horror. My whole world turned desolate. I ran over without a word, cradled PLT tenderly in my arms and carried her upstairs. Placing her on my bed, I wrapped my mortally wounded pet in my best school scarf and lay down next to her. It was a night of grief I have never forgotten.

I lay there with my eyes closed pretending to be asleep but was actually hopelessly awake. Surely everything would remain the same as long as I kept my eyes shut and did not look at PLT. Perhaps, when I finally opened them again after wishing very hard all night, PLT's leg would miraculously be healed.

Though it was the height of summer and Aunt Baba had lowered the mosquito net over my bed, I was deathly cold; thinking over and over, 'When tomorrow comes, will PLT be all right?'

In spite of everything, I must have dozed off because at the break of dawn I woke up with a jerk. Beside me, PLT was now completely still. The horrors of the previous evening flooded back and everything was as bad as before. Worse, because PLT was now irrevocably dead. Gone forever.

Almost immediately, I heard Father calling Jackie in the garden. He was preparing to take his dog for their customary Sunday morning walk. At the sound of Jackie's bark, Aunt Baba suddenly sat up in her bed. 'Quick! Take this opportunity while Jackie's away! Run down and bury your pet in the garden. Get the big spade from the tool shed at the back and dig a proper hole.' She handed me an old sewing box, placed PLT's little body inside and closed the lid.

I dashed out of my room and almost collided with Big Brother, who had just come out of the bathroom into the hall.

'Where are *you* going?' he asked, full of curiosity. 'And what's that you're carrying?'

'I'm going to the garden to bury PLT.'

'Bury her! Why don't you give her to Cook and ask him to stew her for breakfast instead? Stewed duck in the evening and stewed duck in the morning! I love the taste of duck, don't you?' He saw the look on my face and knew he had gone too far. 'Look, that was a joke. I didn't really mean it. I'm sorry about last night too. I didn't know which duckling to pick when Father gave me that order. I only took yours because you're the one least likely to give me trouble afterwards. It wasn't anything against you personally, understand?'

'She was my best friend in the whole world…' I began, tears welling up in spite of myself. 'And now I've lost her forever.'

Halfway down the stairs, I heard Third Brother calling from the landing. 'I've been waiting to go to the bathroom but I'll be down in the garden as soon as I can. Don't start without me.'

Key Reading

> ### Autobiography
>
> This text is both an **autobiography** and a **recount**. Its **purpose** is to tell the reader about a series of events – in this case Adeline Yen Mah's early memories.
>
> The main features of this text are:
>
> - It is told in the **first person**, 'I', and the **past tense**, for example, 'I sat stiffly with downcast eyes.'
> - It uses **time connectives**, for example, 'For a moment…'
> - It is usually told in **chronological order**, for example, 'At the break of dawn, I woke up with a jerk.'
> - It includes **specific facts** from the writer's past, for example, the names of her family – Big Brother, Aunt Baba.
> - It includes **personal feelings**, for example, 'I was overwhelmed with horror'

1 Why is paragraph 5, in which Adeline stays with her pet all night, particularly poignant?

2 Identify the powerful words and images that express Adeline's feelings in the following passage:

> I ran over without a word, cradled PLT tenderly in my arms and carried her upstairs. Placing her on the bed, I wrapped my mortally wounded pet in my best school scarf and lay down next to her.

3 Adeline's feelings about her father are likely to be complex. What do you think some of them might be?

4 Write a short comment (about 30 words) saying how you as the reader react to this episode from Adeline's autobiography.

Purpose

5 In later life Adeline rises above her unhappy childhood. How might writing her autobiography have helped?

R6 **6** Adeline dedicates her book to 'all unwanted children', and in the preface she writes:

> *Chinese Cinderella* is my autobiography. It was difficult and painful to write but I felt compelled to do so. Though mine is but a simple, personal tale of my childhood, please do not underestimate the power of such stories. In one way or another every one of us has been shaped and moulded by the stories we have read and absorbed in the past. All stories, including fairy-tales, present elemental truths which can sometimes permeate your inner life and become part of you.

a) What does this tell you about Adeline's purpose in writing her autobiography?

b) Some authors do not include a dedication or a preface. Why has Adeline done so?

7 What do you think are the essential ingredients of a good autobiography?

Reading for meaning

There are several powerful descriptions in the passage. For example, PLT as:

> a… defenceless creature beset with perils

W7

8 Sometimes a powerful description or statement about one thing can tell us about another. In what sense is this true of the above quotation?

9 a) Through Adeline's recount of events we can infer a great deal about others' attitudes to her. Find the following lines in the extract. What does each reveal about the character who is speaking or being referred to?
- 'She… placed PLT's little body inside and closed the lid.'
- 'Why don't you give her to Cook…?'
- 'She was my best friend in the whole world…'
- 'Don't start without me.'

b) Now write a paragraph (about 200 words) commenting on:
- Adeline's position in the family
- how she is treated by different members of her family.

Quote from some of the statements above to support your comments.

Focus on: Structure

There are three parts to the structure of the extract. They follow in sequence.

The first part is the death of PLT.

10 a) What are the others? Identify which paragraphs are included in each part.

b) Create a timeline and make notes showing the sequence of events in the recount.

11 Events in a recount do not need to be sequenced in time order. The writer could have begun at the end, describing the burial of PLT, and then recounted the previous events.

Think of other ways the recount could have begun, and record your ideas.

Exploring further: Subjectivity in autobiography

Autobiographies are based on truth, but not all memories are reliable. Furthermore, those who witness the same events have different perspectives. While we can assume that the events described in the text occurred, we do not know how different Adeline's relations' memories of them might be.

12 a) In pairs, discuss whether or not it matters that autobiography is subjective.

b) We could say that there is 'a greater truth' in the text that is not dependant on other people's accounts. What do you think this 'truth' is in the case of this extract? Explore several possibilities.

Key Writing

13 Choose from one of the following options for your written work:

A

Rewrite the events from Aunt Baba's point of view, and change the structure. (For example, you could begin at the end and then go back in time.) Think about Aunt Baba's concern for Adeline. Include speech and write a preface (as Aunt Baba) to go with the extract.
Remember: Aunt Baba will not have witnessed every scene (such as the exchange between Adeline and Big Brother), so adapt your writing to fit.

B

Adeline Yen Mah writes that we are all 'shaped and moulded by the stories we have read and absorbed in the past'. These may be fictional or true. Create a powerful story about an incident from your childhood. It could be similar to the incident in the extract. You could draw on your own experience or it could be entirely imaginary. If so, you could use a picture or photograph (for example, from a newspaper) as a stimulus.

Remember to:
- use time connectives to show the course of your recount
- include specific detail
- write in the first person and past tense
- experiment with the structure (for example, you could begin at the end or shift back and forth in time).

4 Unit 9 Assignment: The journalist

Assessment Focus

- AF2 Produce texts which are appropriate to task, reader and purpose
- AF4 Construct paragraphs and use cohesion within and between paragraphs

> **You:** are a journalist.
>
> **Your task:** to write a discursive article for a school magazine discussing the issue of boys' underachievement. You will also discuss why you think girls achieve.

Stage 1

Remember, when you write a discursive account you consider the issue through a number of different arguments.

Create a plan for the main part of your article by copying down the headings below. Then quickly refer back to your notes from pages 200-203 and write down the issue and arguments.

> The issue:
> Boys' underachievement – Argument 1:
> Boys' underachievement – Argument 2:
> Girls' achievement at school – Argument 3:

Make sure you understand all three main arguments.

Stage 2

Again using your notes, highlight or underline the main points and the evidence for each argument.

For example, Argument 1 might begin:

'The changes boys undergo in adolescence make them...'

Add the evidence to your plan. What other points and evidence would you highlight?

Repeat this process for Argument 2. Remember, it is opposed to Argument 1.

Finally, go through the same process for Argument 3, giving reasons for girls' success at school.

Complete your plan by adding notes for:
- an opening statement that introduces the issue
- a conclusion in which you weigh up the arguments.

Stage 3

Use your plan either:
- to consider Arguments 1, 2 and 3 in turn

or:
- to address Arguments 1 and 2 together – making one or two points about one argument, then one or two about the other, showing the differences or similarities, if there are any. Carry on in this way, back and forth, until you have covered all your points.
  Argument 3 can either be integrated in a similar way or presented separately at the end of the article.

Whichever structure you choose, remember to include:
- a brief opening statement about the issue
- evidence to support Arguments 1, 2 and 3
- a range of connectives
- formal language, including the passive if appropriate
- a short conclusion about the issue and arguments put forward, which may include your personal view.

Unit 10 Practising for assessment

Aims

- Find out more about testing in English and how to do your best
- Practise some skills related to test and assessment work

Why are students assessed?

It is important for you, your teachers, and your parents to know what you can do well, and what you need more help with. For example, questions can test how well you have read and understood a text.

Look at the extract below. It comes from the mock Reading Paper your teacher will give you to practise for the Key Stage 3 Test. The text is about Microsoft's plans to develop the human body as a communication device.

> Call it the ultimate wireless network. From the ends of your fingers to the tips of your toes, the human body is a moving, throbbing collection of tubes and tunnels, filled with salty water and all capable of transmitting the lifeblood of the 21st century: information.

Here are two questions you might be asked about the extract above:

1) What is a 'moving, throbbing collection of tubes and tunnels'?
2) What words or phrases does the writer use to paint a vivid picture of the human body?

1 a) Which of the two questions on page 212 do you think is more difficult? Think about:
- which one asks you for a single answer
- which one asks you to make a judgement by looking at several things.

b) Try to answer the questions.

The questions are designed to test different levels of understanding in reading skills. That is the point of the test.

Why don't teachers just look at class and homework?

It is good practice to get used to these tests, since you will have to do tests at GCSE and beyond. Your teacher can then also be sure that you and the rest of the class have complete the assessment under the same conditions.

What is the real Key Stage 3 English Test like?

There are **three** papers (or parts of the test).

The Reading Paper

- This paper consists of three different texts/extracts (for example, these could be an extract from a story, a report, and an advertisement or leaflet).
- It also has questions on each text.
- It is worth **32 marks**.
- You have **1 hour 15 minutes** to read the extracts and answer the questions.

The Writing Paper

There are **two** writing tasks.

Section A contains the longer writing task. This asks you to write a well-developed response on a set topic. There is also a plan to help you.

- It is worth **30 marks**.
- You have **45 minutes** to complete the task (this includes 15 minutes planning time).

Section B contains the shorter writing task. The focus here is on writing a precise, focused, shorter piece of writing in response to a set topic. There is no planning frame to support you.

- It is worth **20 marks**, including 4 for spelling.
- You have **30 minutes** to complete the task.

The Shakespeare Paper

This includes **two** extracts from the set scenes from the play you are studying.

- It includes one task that tests your knowledge and understanding of the play.
- It is worth **18 marks**.
- It is based on the two scenes you have studied in detail.
- You have **45 minutes** to complete the paper.

Total marks for the Test:

Reading:	Reading Paper	32
	Shakespeare Paper	18
Writing:	Longer writing task	30
	Shorter writing task	20
TOTAL marks:		100

Advice on the Reading Test

You will be assessed on **five** different areas.

1. **Your ability to *understand, describe, select or retrieve information from texts***

    This means looking at the text you have been given, then finding information you have been asked for. Sometimes you will be asked to explain this information.

2. **Your ability to *deduce, infer or interpret information***

   This means explaining something from the text that might not be so obvious, for example, where a writer suggests something, but doesn't say it directly.

3. **Your ability to *comment on the overall structure of the text***

   This means explaining how the text is organised, for example, saying how the start and end of the text are linked.

4. **Your ability to *explain and comment on the writer's use of language***

   This means explaining how and why the writer chose individual words and phrases.

5. **Your ability to *identify and comment on the writer's purpose and viewpoint, and the overall effect of the text***

   This means explaining what the writer was trying to do, or the point he or she wanted to make, and how effective it was.

Gaining higher levels

According to examiners, the *key* way you can raise your level in order to gain Level 7 is to *analyse in precise ways* how the writer guides what the reader feels or understands when they read the text.

The key word here is 'precise'. You need to make sure any response you give carefully selects the precise word, phrase, or sentence and explains *why* the writer has used it. This is the area in reading that you should especially attend to. For example:

> The use of the verb 'pleaded' clearly shows the writer's strength of feeling.

is better than:

> The writer must feel very strongly because of the way he writes.

Practising Reading Test skills

Skill 1: Reading the question

People always say 'read the question carefully!', but what does that mean? Each question tests a different skill, as you have seen.

Imagine you have just read a leaflet arguing against animal cruelty. Here is a possible question from the test:

> How many cases of animal cruelty are there each year, according to the leaflet? (1 mark)

Let's see what you need to do. First of all, highlight the key words as follows:

Tells us we are looking for a number (of cases)

Tells us that we should look for this, not other types of case

> **How many cases** of **animal cruelty** are there **each year,** according to the leaflet? (1 mark)

Means we should ignore other information about longer periods of time

Pay attention to the marks. Only **one** is available here, so you are likely to be looking for **one** answer or point

2 Highlight the key words in this question:

> Which two types of animal are most likely to be used in animal testing? (2 marks)

Skill 2: Short and long answers

You have already seen how the number of marks can provide guidance when you are answering a reading question, but how else can marks help?

The Reading Test has **32 marks**. You have about one hour to read the questions, search for and write your answers (plus fifteen minutes overall reading time).

This means you have about **two minutes per mark**.

So if a question is worth four marks, you should spend between eight and ten minutes on it (you can speed up on the easier, one mark questions). Of course, you cannot stick to this completely. You will find some questions easier than others, but it does help you stick to the overall time limit.

3 Look back at the text on pages 150–151. Write down two things from the first paragraph that tell us Sipho's family is quite poor. (2 marks)

Remember:
- check the key words in the question
- check the number of marks
- read the text quickly
- try to answer the question as quickly as you can.

A longer question might be:

> How does the writer convey the impression that Sipho's family live in a poor and dangerous neighbourhood? (5 marks)

For a question like this one you would be expected to write a longer answer and probably mention about five different ways or examples, as there are five marks.

4 Try to answer this question in approximately ten minutes.

Practising for assessment

Skill 3: Using evidence

Remember that, in order to attain higher levels in reading, you need to be *precise* in your answer, especially when in the test, you are given questions which ask you to think and give your view, and support it with evidence from the text. You may know the answer but not know how to put it into words or forget to support what you say (with evidence) and just write down what you think.

Look at this sample question, which is also based on the text on pages 150–151.

> Explain how the writer's use of language shows Sipho's fear as he tries to leave. Support your answer with at least two examples.   (2 marks)

An incomplete answer to this question might be:

The writer shows how nervous and frightened Sipho is by the way he acts and moves, and how he is frightened about his stepfather and mother. He uses really good descriptions of how Sipho feels.

A more precise answer would be:

The writer describes how Sipho was 'tiptoeing' around his house, and how he 'held his breath' as he tried to leave. The writer also describes Sipho's heart as being 'as tight as a fist', and this simile suggests the way it is clenched and hard in his chest…

5 Discuss with a partner what is better about the second response.

6 The student uses the word 'describes' twice. Could he or she have used another expression, or reorganised the sentences to make them less similar?

Tip

If you are asked for examples or quotations from the passage, make sure you include them. Look at page 154 for advice on how to use quotations – it does take skill to put them into your sentences.

Skill 4: Reading between the lines

This skill is more difficult, because you have to use your judgement and look under the surface to explain something. It is about making inferences and interpreting what the writer says. Read the following text:

> The hotel had swirly, highly-coloured wallpaper and a musty sort of smell which some people would have considered old-fashioned, charming and quaint. The meals were 'traditional' – that's to say, extremely well-cooked, very British, and with enormous portions – especially of sprouts. Lovely, if you like that kind of thing.

The writer does not say **directly** that he doesn't like the hotel, but he **implies** it by:

- using the phrase 'some people' – implies that he is not one of the people who would like the smell and the wallpaper
- using quotation marks around 'traditional' as if to suggest it is out-of-date and boring.

7 a) How does the writer imply that he doesn't like the hotel by using **euphemisms**? (Look up this term if necessary.)

  b) How does he imply it through sarcasm?

8 Read the text below. Try to work out what the writer's opinion is and discuss your ideas with a partner.

> The film was action-packed from start to finish with explosions so loud I thought the cinema walls were falling down - not that this bothered the crowds of crisp-crunching, cola-gurgling teenagers who were sitting next to me.
>
> If you want a story with characters and feelings, then this isn't for you. But if you want a film with American accents you can't understand, men with tattoos and bulging muscles who eat their Cornflakes with their guns on the table, and more deaths than World War 2, then this film is definitely your cup of tea – or should I say, blood?

Practising for assessment

Advice on the Writing Test

The Writing Test contains **two** tasks – a longer task, and a shorter one. The key skills assessed are:

The shorter writing task

1. Sentence structure, punctuation and text organisation

This is the way your sentences are put together: the accuracy and effect of your use of punctuation; the way your writing fits together – how it makes sense and how it is organised, for example, whether your paragraphs help the reader to follow your line of thought.

2. Composition and effect

This means the particular choices of words and phrases to fit the sort of text you are writing – for example, powerful description for narrative stories, clear vocabulary for advice texts, etc.; how well you interest the reader.

3. Spelling

This means how well you spell words you are expected to know at your age, and tackle more difficult, complex or unfamiliar words. Spelling is not specifically assessed on the longer writing task.

The longer writing task

1. Sentence structure and punctuation

This means how clearly organised, fluent and effective your sentences are. Ask yourself:

- Have you used a variety of sentence structures (i.e. long, short, simple, complex) to fit the task?
- Have you used suitable connectives (joining words and phrases, such as 'however', 'despite' or 'in addition') to link sentences?

- Have you used a variety of verbs and verb forms to suit the writing task, for example, suitable tenses or modals such as 'should', 'may' or 'might'?
- Have you used punctuation (full-stops, commas, semicolons) to make meaning clear or for effect (for example, exclamation marks for disbelief: 'I was stunned!')?

2. Text structure and organisation

This means the overall structure and shape of the whole text, and how individual sections or ideas are linked together. Ask yourself:

- Have you written paragraphs with clear links to the subject you are writing about?
- Are your main ideas supported by evidence or other comments or details?
- Have you made the reader follow your line of thought? For example, have you led them towards the point you want to make?
- Have you considered a range of organisational devices, such as bullet points, subheadings or numbering?

3. Composition and effect

This means the appropriate style, form and language for the text you are writing, matched to the purpose of the text and, where relevant, the viewpoint of the writer. Ask yourself:

- Does your style match the form of the text (for example, if this is a formal business report, a chatty, personal style would not be suitable)? Have you kept this style throughout your piece?
- Have you shaped your writing to suit the reader? For example, if you need to make an impact, have you used original ideas or language?
- Have you used a suitable range of vocabulary – words, phrases and sentences – to fit the form (for example, in a report you might write, 'I have concluded from my analysis of the situation…')?

Use the bullet points above as a guide when completing the mock Writing Tests.

Gaining higher levels

Examiners suggest many ways of gaining a Level 7 in writing. Two of the key ways are:

- By providing implicit links between paragraphs in a smooth, fluent way. This means that you don't always have to say: 'My next point is…' in a very *obvious* way, but can signal a new idea more subtly. For example, there is no need for a *link* word in this example:

> The upshot is, we need to write to all parents immediately. We need to make it clear: bad behaviour will not be tolerated, in this school – or in any other.

- By using a variety of types of punctuation in a creative way, consciously making meaning and creating effect. Note the brackets and the last sentence in this example:

> The food was as tasteless as the wallpaper (and I don't mean to look at), and the waiter was the embodiment of those three vices: speaking to you when you wanted to be left alone; late with the food he did bring; and expecting a large tip for pretending to care about your needs.

Advice on the Shakespeare Paper

The Shakespeare Paper is a reading assessment, and therefore assesses the same basic areas as for the main Reading Paper. Below is a broad reminder of what is required.

The Play: You will have read and studied one play by Shakespeare. There are **two or three scenes** which you will prepare before the test, extracts from which appear in the Shakespeare Paper.

The Test: There is **one** task, which tests your knowledge and understanding of the play. It is worth **18 marks** and is based on the set scenes you have studied in detail. You have **45 minutes** to complete the test.

Preparation: The following exercises will help you prepare for the test.

- Describe the plot (the story) of the play to a friend in less than two minutes. Your friend should stop and correct you if you forget a key character or event.
- Write the name of a main character in the middle of an A4 sheet. Draw lines from that character and add at the end of each one another character and how they are connected.
- Write down the key themes from the play (such as ambition, love, disguise) on a set of postcards. Then write down a quotation from the play that matches the theme on one side, and one or two events that match the theme on the other side.
- Read one of your key scenes with a group of friends. Try to act out a basic version of the scene (in your own words) in five minutes.
- On your own, walk around your bedroom, kitchen or garden reading the lines from your key scenes aloud – this will help you get a sense of the sound and feeling of the language.

Gaining higher levels

Examiners say that too often students ignore the *dramatic effect* of characters' words and actions. This means that they are generally good at describing a character and why he or she acts in a particular way, but forget that this is a *play*.

9 Look at the example below. How is 'dramatic effect' suggested?

> When she faints, her action would draw the audience to her, as much as the other characters on the stage, and in this way she temporarily takes our minds, as well as the other characters', off the murder.

William Collins' dream of knowledge for all began with the publication of his first book in 1819. A self-educated mill worker, he not only enriched millions of lives, but also founded a flourishing publishing house. Today, staying true to this spirit, Collin packed with inspiration, innovation and practical expertise. They place you at the centre of a world of possibility and give you exactly what you need to explore it.

Collins. Do more.

Published by Collins
An imprint of HarperCollins*Publishers*
77–85 Fulham Palace Road
Hammersmith
London
W6 8JB

Browse the complete Collins catalogue at
www.collinseducation.com

© HarperCollins*Publishers* Limited 2005

10 9 8 7 6 5 4 3 2 1

ISBN 0 00 719516 8

Mike Gould, Mary Green, John Mannion and Kim Richardson assert their moral rights to be identified as the authors of this work

All rights reserved. No part of this publication may be reproduced, stored in a retrieval system, or transmitted in any form or by any means, electronic, mechanical, photocopying, recording or otherwise, without the prior written permission of the Publisher or a licence permitting restricted copying in the United Kingdom issued by the Copyright Licensing Agency Ltd., 90 Tottenham Court Road, London W1T 4LP.

British Library Cataloguing in Publication Data
A Catalogue record for this publication is available from the British Library

Acknowledgements

The following permissions to reproduce material are gratefully acknowledged:

Text: Extract from 'The Mazarin Stone' taken from *The Case-Book of Sherlock Holmes* by Sir Arthur Conan Doyle, pp4–5; extract from *Master of the Rings: Inside the World of J.R.R. Tolkien* by Susan Ang (Wizard Books, 2002), pp11–12; review of 'Catch me if you can' from channel4.com, pp18–19; extract from *The Mother Tongue* by Bill Bryson (Penguin Books, 1991), pp26–27; 'Online words take wing' from *The Sunday Times*, pp33–34; extract from *Eats, Shoots & Leaves: The Zero Tolerance Approach to Punctuation* by Lynne Truss (Profile Books, 2003), pp40–41; extract from *The Complete Idiot's Guide to Elvis* by Frank Coffey (Alpha Books, 1997), pp48–49; inauguration speech by Nelson Mandela extracted from *In His Own Words*, edited by Kader Asmal and David Chidester (Little Brown and Company, 2003), pp55–56; 'The Kinnock Maiden Speech in Full' from *Private Eye*, 12 November 2004, pp56; 'How to write a letter to someone famous from justdosomething.net, pp62–63; 'On the eighth day' by Claire Calman © Claire Calman 2000 from *The Pop! Anthology (New Departures 2000)* edited by Michael Horovitz and Inge Elsa Laird, pp72–73; extract from 'Of Jeoffrey, His Cat' by Christopher Smart, p77; 'When we two parted' by Lord Byron, pp79–80; 'Anancy's Thoughts on Love' by John Agard from *Touchstones 5*, edited by Michael Benton and Peter Benton (Hodder and Stoughton, 1988), p81; 'Homeward Bound' and 'Neighbours' by Benjamin Zephaniah from *Propa Propaganda* (Bloodaxe Books, 2000) © Benjamin Zephaniah 1996, pp87–89; extract from *Stone Cold: The Play* by Joe Standerline, based on the novel by Robert Swindells (Nelson Thornes, 1999), pp98–100; Thames Reach Bondway poster and website reproduced with permission. Copy by Jeremy Swain, pp104–106; extract from *As I Walked Out One Midsummer Morning* by Laurie Lee (Penguin, 1971), pp111–112; 'Katie believes in God and marriage. Her mother doesn't' by Liz Lightfoot, from the *Daily Telegraph*, 11 March 2004, pp122–123; 'How to...go to a party' by Guy Browning from *The Guardian*, 4 October 2003, pp136–137; 'Letter to Daniel' by Fergal Keane, first broadcast on BBC Radio4, February 1996, pp144–145; extract from *No Turning Back* by Beverly Naidoo (Penguin, 2004), pp150–151; 'Tiger tracking in Rajasthan' from *Nature Journeys* by Dwight Holing (Weldon Owen Inc, 1996), pp156–157; extract from *The Woman in Black* by Susan Hill (Vintage, 1998), pp166–167; 'What is a phobia' from pe2000.com, pp173–174; extract from *To Kill a Mockingbird: Play* by Christopher Sergal, based on the novel by Harper Lee (Heinemann, 1995), pp179–181; extract from *To Kill a Mockingbird* by Harper Lee (Heinemann, 1960), p185; extract from *The Lost Boys' Appreciation Society* by Alan Gibbons (Orion Children's Books, 2004), pp190–191; extract from *Chinese Cinderella* by Adeline Yen Mah (Penguin, 1999), pp204–205, 207.

Images: Alamy: pp66, 89, 146; Aquarius: pp19, 23; Tim Archbold, Graham Cameron Illustration: pp73, 74, 77; Ardea: 157, 159, 173, 177; Corbis: pp51, 88, 134, 149, 155, 169; Bob Farley: Graham Cameron Illustration: pp5, 7, 24; Getty Images: pp17, 32, 36, 49, 53, 56, 60, 62, 69, 92, 110, 115, 118, 123, 125, 129, 138, 141, 143, 160, 164, 188, 195, 198, 207, 210; Robert Harding: p113; Moviestore: pp12, 14, 41, 181, 186; Nicola Taylor, NB Illustration: 80, 81, 96.

Whilst every effort has been made both to contact the copyright holders and to give exact credit lines, this has not proved possible in every case.

Printed and bound by Printing Express, Hong Kong